作 者 近 照

Recent Photo of the Author

旋法至極

佛法無邊　　　　　　法輪常轉

This Falun emblem is the miniature of the universe. It also has its own form of existence and process of evolution in all other dimensions; therefore, I call it a world.

Li Hongzhi

FALUN GONG
(REVISED EDITION)

(ENGLISH VERSION)

LI HONGZHI

ISBN: 1-58613-100-1

Third Translation Edition (March, 2000. USA)

Published by The Universe Publishing Company

Printed in the United States of America

LUNYU[1]

"The Buddha Fa"[2] is most profound; among all the theories in the world, it is the most intricate and extraordinary science. In order to explore this domain, humankind must fundamentally change its conventional thinking. Otherwise, the truth of the universe will forever remain a mystery to humankind, and everyday people will forever crawl within the boundary delimited by their own ignorance.

Then what exactly is "the Buddha Fa"? Is it a religion? Is it a philosophy? That is only the understanding of the "modernized Buddhist scholars," who merely study theories. They regard it as a philosophical category for critical studies and so-called research. Actually, "the Buddha Fa" is not only the tiny portion documented in the scriptures, for that is simply "the Buddha Fa" at an elementary level. "The Buddha Fa" is an insight into all mysteries. It encompasses everything and leaves out nothing—from particles and molecules to the universe, from the even smaller to the even greater. It is an exposition of the characteristics of the universe, "Zhen, Shan, and Ren,"[3] expressed at different levels with different layers of meaning. It is also what the Tao School calls the "Tao,"[4] or what the Buddha School calls the "Fa."[5]

---

[1] Lunyu (loon-yew)—statement; comment.

[2] the Buddha Fa—the universal principles and law; the way of the universe.

[3] Zhen (jhun), Shan (shahn) and Ren (ren)—Zhen (truth, truthfulness); Shan (compassion, benevolence, kindness); Ren (forbearance, tolerance, endurance).

[4] Tao—1. also known as "Dao," Taoist term for "the Way of nature and the universe"; 2. enlightened being who has achieved this Tao.

[5] Fa (fah)—law and principles in the Buddha School.

As advanced as the present human science has become, it is still only part of the mysteries of the universe. Whenever we mention specific phenomena of "the Buddha Fa," someone will claim: "This is already the electronic age, and science is very advanced. Spaceships have already flown to other planets, yet you still bring up these outdated superstitions." To put it frankly, no matter how advanced a computer is, it is still no match for the human brain, which to this day remains an unfathomable enigma. However far a spaceship may fly, it cannot travel beyond this physical dimension in which our human race exists. What can be understood with modern human knowledge is extremely shallow and tiny; it is far from truly coming to terms with the truth of the universe. Some people even dare not face, touch upon, or admit the facts of phenomena that objectively exist, because they are too conservative and unwilling to change their conventional thinking. Only through "the Buddha Fa," can the mysteries of the universe, time-space, and the human body be completely unveiled. It is able to truly distinguish what is righteous from evil, good from bad, and eliminate all misconceptions while providing what is correct.

The guiding ideology for today's human science is confined only to this physical world in its research and development, as a subject will not be studied until it is recognized—it follows such a path. As for phenomena that are intangible and invisible in our dimension, but objectively exist and are reflected into our physical dimension as concrete manifestations, people dare not approach them, dismissing them as unknown phenomena. Opinionated people groundlessly try to reason that they are natural phenomena, while those with ulterior motives, against their own conscience, simply label all of them as superstition. Those who are indifferent simply stay away from the issue with the excuse that science is not yet advanced enough. If human beings are able to take a fresh look at themselves as well as the universe and change their rigid mentalities, humankind will make a leap forward. "The Buddha Fa" enables humankind to understand the immeasurable and boundless world. Throughout the ages, only "the Buddha Fa" has been able to perfectly provide a clear exposition of humanity, every dimension of material existence, life, and the entire universe.

Contents

Chapter I Introduction 1

1. The Origins of Qigong 2

2. Qi and Gong 5

3. Energy Potency and Supernormal Abilities 6
   (1) Energy Potency is Developed through
       Cultivation of Xinxing *(Mind Nature)* 6
   (2) Supernormal Abilities are Not What
       Cultivators Pursue 7
   (3) Handling of Energy Potency 9

4. Tianmu *(The Third Eye)* 11
   (1) Opening Tianmu 11
   (2) Tianmu's Levels 13
   (3) Remote Sight 16
   (4) Dimensions 17

5. Qigong Treatments and Hospital Treatments 19

6. Qigong of the Buddha School and Buddhism 22
   (1) Qigong of the Buddha School 23
   (2) Buddhism 24

7. Righteous Cultivation Ways and Evil Ways 26
   (1) The Side-Door Clumsy Way *(Pangmen Zuodao)* 26
   (2) Martial Arts Qigong 27
   (3) Reverse Cultivation and Energy Borrowing 28
   (4) Cosmic Language 30
   (5) Spirit Possession 31
   (6) An Evil Way can be Produced in Righteous Practice . 32

Chapter II Falun Gong **33**

1. Falun's Function 33

2. Falun's Configuration 36

3. Characteristics of Falun Gong Cultivation 37
   (1) The Fa Refines the Practitioner 37
   (2) Cultivation of Main Consciousness 39
   (3) Cultivate Regardless of Direction and Time 41

4. Cultivation of Both Mind and Body 42
   (1) Changing Benti 42
   (2) The Falun Heavenly Circuit 44
   (3) Opening the Meridians 46

5. Mind-intent 47

6. Levels of Cultivation in Falun Gong 49
   (1) Cultivation at Higher Levels 49
   (2) Gong's Manifestations 50
   (3) Beyond-Triple-World-Law Cultivation 51

Chapter III Cultivation of Xinxing **53**

1. Xinxing's Inner Meaning 53

2. Loss and Gain 55

3. Simultaneous Cultivation of Zhen, Shan, and Ren 59

4. Eliminating Jealousy 61

5. Abandoning Attachments 63

6. Karma 65
   (1) The Origin of Karma 65
   (2) Eliminating Karma 68

7. Demonic Interference 72

8. Inborn Quality and Enlightenment Quality 74

9. A Clear and Clean Mind 77

Chapter IV Falun Gong Practice System 81

1. Buddha Showing A Thousand Hands Exercise 82

2. The Falun Standing Stance Exercise 95

3. Penetrating the Two Cosmic Extremes Exercise 100

4. Falun Heavenly Circuit Exercise 106

5. Strengthening Divine Powers Exercise 114

Some Basic Requirements and Words of Caution
    for Practicing Falun Gong 125

Chapter V Questions and Answers 128

1. Falun and Falun Gong 128

2. Practice Principles and Methods 134

3. Cultivating Xinxing 162

4. Tianmu 170

5. Tribulations 180

6. Dimensions and Humankind 183

Chapter I

Introduction

In our country, [China], *qigong¹* dates back to ancient times and has a long history. Our people thus have a natural advantage in practicing qigong. As the sanctioned methods of cultivation, the two qigong schools of Buddha and Tao have made public many great cultivation ways that were previously taught in private. The way of cultivation in the Tao School is very unique, while the Buddha School also has its own cultivation method. Falun² Gong is an advanced cultivation method of the Buddha School. In class, I will first adjust your body, putting it into a state suitable for advanced cultivation, and I will then install Falun and energy mechanisms in your body. I will also teach you the exercises. In addition to all of these, I have Law Bodies *(fashen)³* who will protect you. But having only these things is inadequate, as they cannot achieve the goal of developing *gong⁴* —it is necessary that you also understand the principles for cultivation at higher levels. This is what this book is going to address.

I am teaching gong at higher levels, so I won't discuss cultivation of any particular channel, acupuncture point, or energy passage. I am teaching the Great Way *(Dafa)* of cultivation, the Dafa for true cultivation toward higher levels. Initially it may sound inconceivable. But as long as those who are dedicated to practicing qigong carefully explore and experience it, they will

---

¹ *qigong* (chee-gong)—a form of traditional Chinese practice which cultivates qi or "vital energy."

² Falun (fah-luhn)—Law Wheel.

³ *fashen* (fah-shun)—"law body"; a body made of gong and Fa.

⁴ *gong* (gong)—1. cultivation energy; 2. practice that cultivates such energy.

1

find all the wonders and intricacies within it.

1. The Origins of Qigong

The qigong that we refer to today was not, in fact, originally called qigong. It originated from solitary cultivation by the ancient Chinese and from cultivation in religions. The two-character term, "qi gong," is nowhere to be found in the texts of Dan Jing, Tao Zang,[5] and the Tripitaka.[6] During the course of development in our present human civilization, qigong has passed through the period when religions were in their embryonic forms. It had already been in existence before religions formed. After religions formed, it was somewhat colored by religion. Qigong's original names were "The Great Cultivation Way of Buddha," and "The Great Cultivation Way of Tao." It had additional names, such as "Nine-fold Internal Alchemy," "The Way of Arhat," "The Dhyana of Vajra," etc. We now call it "qigong" so that it better suits our modern ideology and is more easily popularized in society. Qigong is, in fact, something existing in China that is purely for the purpose of cultivating the human body.

Qigong is not something invented by this civilization. It has a fairly long history, dating back to distant years. So when did qigong come into being? Some say that qigong has a history of three thousand years, and it was very popular during the Tang Dynasty.[7] Some say it has a history of five thousand years—as

---

[5] Dan Jing (dahn jing), Tao Tsang (daow zang)—classic Chinese texts of cultivation practice.

[6] Tripitaka—a Buddhist scripture.

[7] Tang (tahng) Dynasty—one of the most prosperous periods in Chinese history (618 A.D.-907 A.D.).

2

old as Chinese civilization. Judging from archeological findings, some say it already has a history of seven thousand years. I regard qigong as something not invented by modern humankind—it is prehistoric culture. According to investigations by people with supernormal abilities, the universe we live in is an entity that was recombined after its being exploded nine times. The planet we dwell on has been destroyed many times. Each time, after the planet has been reassembled, humankind has again started to multiply. At present, we have discovered already that there are many things in the world that surpass the present civilization. According to Darwin's theory of evolution, humans evolved from apes and civilization is no more than ten thousand years old. Yet archaeological findings have revealed that in the caves of the European Alps there exist 250 thousand-year-old frescoes that exhibit a very high level of artistry—one far beyond the abilities of modern people. In the museum of the National University of Peru, there is a large rock on which a figure is engraved, holding a telescope and observing the celestial bodies. This figure is more than thirty thousand years old. As we know it, Galileo invented a 30X astronomical telescope in 1609, just over three hundred years ago. How could there have been a telescope thirty thousand years ago? There is an iron pillar in India of which the iron content is over ninety-nine percent. Even modern smelting technology cannot produce iron with such high purity; it already surpasses the level of modern technology. Who created those civilizations? How could human beings—who would have been microorganisms in those times—create these things? These discoveries have caught the attention of scientists worldwide. Since they prove inexplicable, they are called "prehistoric culture."

The scientific level has been different in each time period. In some time periods it was quite high, surpassing that of our modern humankind. But those civilizations were destroyed. Therefore, I say that qigong wasn't invented or created by modern people, but discovered and perfected by modern people. It is prehistoric culture.

Actually, qigong isn't a product exclusive to our country. It exists in foreign countries as well, but they don't call it qigong. Western countries, such as the United States, Great Britain, etc., call it magic. David Copperfield, a magician in the US, is a master of supernormal abilities, and he once performed the feat of walking through the Great Wall of China. When he was about to pass through the Wall, he used a white cloth as a cover, applied himself to the Wall, and then proceeded to go through it. Why did he do that? That way, many people would consider it a magic performance. It had to be done that way, for he knew that there were many people with great supernormal abilities in China. He was afraid of interference from them, so he covered himself before he went in. When coming out, he stuck one hand out, raised the cloth, and walked out. "Experts watch for tricks while laymen watch for excitement."[8] This way, the audience thought it was a magic performance. These supernormal abilities are called "magic" because they are not used to cultivate the human body, but to perform miracles and entertain through stage performances. At a low level, qigong can change the condition of one's body, achieving the goals of healing and fitness. At a higher level, qigong refers to cultivation of *benti*.[9]

---

[8] "Experts watch for tricks while laymen watch for excitement."—a Chinese saying.

[9] *benti* (bun-tee)—one's physical body and the bodies in other dimensions.

2. Qi and Gong

The *qi*[10] we now talk about was called *chi* by ancient people. They are essentially the same, as both refer to the qi of the universe—a shapeless, invisible kind of substance throughout the universe. "Qi" does not refer to air. Through cultivation, the energy of this substance will be activated in the human body, changing the body's physical state, having the effects of healing and making one fit. Yet qi is merely qi—you have qi, he has qi, and one's qi cannot have a restraining effect on another's qi. Some say that qi can cure disease, or that you can emit qi towards someone to cure his disease. These remarks are very unscientific, because qi cannot cure disease whatsoever. When a practitioner's body still possesses qi, it means that his body isn't yet a Milk-White Body. That is, he might still have disease.

A person who, through practice, possesses advanced capabilities does not emit qi. Instead, he emits a high-energy cluster. This is a high-energy substance that manifests in the form of light, with fine particles and high density. This is gong. Only this can have a restraining effect on everyday people, and only this can heal their ailments. There is a saying, "The Buddha's light illuminates everywhere and rectifies all abnormalities." It means that those who practice true cultivation carry immense energy in their bodies. Wherever such a person passes, any abnormal condition within the area covered by his energy can be corrected and restored to normal. For instance, sickness in one's body is indeed an abnormal bodily state, and illness will disappear after this condition is corrected. More plainly put, gong is energy. Gong has physical characteristics; practitioners can, through cultivation, experience and perceive its existence.

[10] *qi* (chee)—In Chinese culture, it is believed to be "vital energy"; but compared to gong, it is a lower form of energy.

5

3. Energy Potency and Supernormal Abilities

(1) Energy Potency is Developed through Cultivation of Xinxing[11]

The gong that truly determines the level of one's energy potency is not developed through practicing exercises. It is developed through the transformation of the substance *de,*[12] and through the cultivation of *xinxing*. This conversion process isn't accomplished by "setting up the crucible and furnace to cultivate *dan*[13] from gathered medical drugs,"[14] as imagined by everyday people. The gong we refer to is generated outside the body, and it begins from the lower half of the body. Following the improvement of xinxing, it grows upward in spiral shape, being formed completely outside one's body. Next, when reaching the crown of the head it develops into an energy column. The energy column's height determines the level of a person's gong. The energy column exists in a deeply hidden dimension, making it difficult for an average person to see.

Supernormal abilities are strengthened by energy potency. The higher the energy potency and the higher a person's level, the greater his supernormal abilities are and the easier their usage. People with a lower energy potency have weaker supernormal abilities; they find it harder to apply them, and some are completely unusable. Supernormal abilities themselves represent neither the level of one's energy potency, nor one's cultivation level. What determines one's level is energy potency, rather than supernormal abilities. Some people cultivate in a "locked" mode, whereby their energy potency is very high but they cannot display many

---

[11] *xinxing* (shin-shing)—mind or heart nature; moral character.

[12] *de* (duh)—"virtue" or "merit"; a white substance.

[13] *dan* (dahn)—energy cluster in a cultivator's body, collected from other dimensions.

[14] A Taoist metaphor for internal alchemy.

supernormal abilities. Energy potency is the determining factor, and it is developed through xinxing cultivation. This is the most crucial.

(2) Supernormal Abilities are Not What Cultivators Pursue

All practitioners care about supernormal abilities. In society, supernatural abilities are attractive and many people want to acquire some. But without good xinxing, one won't be able to acquire these supernormal abilities.

Some supernormal abilities may be had by everyday people, including an open *tianmu*,[15] clairaudience, telepathy, precognition, etc. But not all of these supernormal abilities will appear during the stage of gradual enlightenment, as they vary with each individual. It is impossible for everyday people to have certain supernormal abilities, such as transforming one kind of substance in this physical dimension to another kind of substance—this isn't something everyday people can have. Great supernormal abilities are developed only through cultivation after birth. Falun Gong was developed based on the principles of the universe, so all supernormal abilities that exist in the universe exist in Falun Gong. It all depends on how practitioners cultivate. The thought of acquiring some supernormal abilities isn't considered wrong. Nevertheless, excessively intense pursuit is more than a normal thought, and it will produce negative results. It is of little use for one to acquire supernormal abilities at a lower level, save for trying to employ these to show off one's abilities in front of everyday people, becoming the stronger one among them. If this is the case, it indicates precisely that one's xinxing is not high and that it is right not to give him supernormal abilities. If given

---

[15] *tianmu* (tyen-moo)—"heavenly eye," also known as the "third eye."

to people with bad xinxing, some supernormal abilities can be used to commit wrongdoing. Because such people's xinxing are not steady, there is no guarantee that they won't do something bad.

On the other hand, any supernormal abilities that can be shown or performed cannot change human society or alter normal social life. Real high-level supernormal abilities are not allowed to be taken out for performance, because the impact and danger would be too great; for example, one will never perform pulling down a large building. Except for people with special missions, great supernormal abilities are not allowed to be used, and neither can they be revealed; it is because they are restrained by high-level masters.

Yet some everyday people insist on having qigong masters perform, forcing them to display their supernormal abilities. People with supernormal abilities are unwilling to use them for performance, since they are forbidden to reveal them; displaying them would impact the entire state of society. People who genuinely possess great de are not allowed to use their supernormal abilities in public. Some qigong masters feel awful during a performance, and want to cry afterward. Don't force them to perform! It is upsetting to them to reveal these things. A student brought a magazine to me. I felt disgusted the moment I read it. It mentioned that an international qigong conference was to be held. People with supernormal abilities could participate in a contest, and whoever had the greatest supernormal abilities could go to that conference. After I read it I felt upset for days. Supernormal abilities are not something that can be publicly displayed for competition—showing them in public is regrettable. Everyday people focus on practical things in the mundane world, but qigong masters must have dignity.

What is the motive behind wanting supernormal abilities? It reflects a practitioner's realm of mind and his pursuits. With impure pursuits and an unreliable mind, he is unlikely to have great supernormal abilities. This is because before you are fully enlightened, what you see as good or bad is only based on the standards of this world. You can see neither the true nature of things, nor the karmic relationships among them. Fighting, scolding, and bullying among people are necessarily caused by karmic relationships. If you cannot perceive them, you can only be more trouble than help. The gratitude and resentment, right and wrong of everyday people are governed by the laws of this world; cultivators shouldn't be concerned with these things. Before you have reached full enlightenment, what you see with your eyes might not necessarily be true. When one person punches another, it might be that they are settling their karmic debts. Your involvement may hamper their settlement. Karma is a type of black substance that surrounds the human body. It has a physical existence in another dimension that can transform into sickness and misfortune.

Everyone possesses supernormal abilities, and the matter is one of developing and strengthening them via continued cultivation. If, as a practitioner, a person only pursues supernormal abilities, he is short sighted and impure in mind. No matter what he wants supernormal abilities for, his pursuit contains elements of selfishness that will definitely hinder cultivation. Consequently, he will never obtain supernormal abilities.

(3) Handling of Energy Potency

Some practitioners haven't practiced for very long, yet they want to treat illness for others to see the effectiveness. For those whose energy potency isn't high, when you extend your hand and try, you absorb into your own body a great deal of black, unhealthy, filthy qi that exists in the patient's body. Since you don't have the ability to resist unhealthy qi and, in addition, your body lacks a protective shield, you form one, shared field with the patient; without high energy potency, you cannot defend against unhealthy qi. As a result, you, yourself will, have a great deal of discomfort. If no one looks after you, over the course of time you will accumulate disease throughout your body. Therefore, one who lacks high energy potency shouldn't treat disease for others. Only a person who has already developed supernormal abilities and possesses a certain level of energy potency can treat disease using qigong. Even though some people have developed supernormal abilities and are able to treat disease, when at a very low level, they are in fact using the accumulated energy potency—their own energy—to treat the disease. Since gong is both energy and an intelligent entity that isn't easily accumulated, emitting gong is actually depleting yourself of it. Accompanying your release of gong, the energy column above your head shortens and is depleted. This is not worth it whatsoever. So I don't endorse treating disease for others when your energy potency isn't high. No matter what methods you use, you will still consume your own energy.

When one's energy potency reaches a certain level, all kinds of supernormal abilities will emerge. You need to be very cautious when using these supernormal abilities. For instance, a person has to use his tianmu when it has opened, since it will close if he never uses it. Yet he shouldn't look through it frequently. If he looks through it too often, too much energy will be discharged. So does this mean one should never use it? Of course not. If we were to never use it, then what's the point of our cultivation practice? The question is when to use it. You may use it only when you have cultivated to a certain stage and possess the ability

10

to replenish yourself. When a cultivator of Falun Gong reaches a certain stage, Falun can automatically transform and replenish however much gong he releases. Falun automatically maintains the level of the energy potency for practitioners, and gong doesn't decrease at any time. This is a characteristic of Falun Gong. Not until this point may supernormal abilities be used.

4. Tianmu

(1) Opening Tianmu

Tianmu's main passage is located between the middle of the forehead and the *shangen*[16] point. The way everyday people see things with the naked eye abides by the same principle as taking pictures with a camera. Depending on the distance of the object and the intensity of light, the size of the lens and pupil are adjusted; images are formed on the pineal body located at the back of the brain via the optic nerves. The supernormal ability of "penetrative sight" is simply the ability of the pineal body to look directly outside through tianmu An average person's tianmu is closed, as the opening of the main passage is very tight and dark. There is no quintessential qi inside, no illumination. Some people's passages are blocked, so they cannot see.

To open tianmu, first we use either outside force or self-cultivation to open the passage. The shape of the passage varies with each individual, ranging from ovular to round, rhombic to triangular. The better you practice, the rounder the passage will become. Second, the master gives you an eye; if you cultivate on your own, then you have to cultivate it yourself. Third, you must

---

[16] *shangen* (shahn-ghun) point—acupuncture point located between one's eyebrows.

11

have the quintessential qi at the place of your tianmu.

We usually see things with our two eyes, and it is exactly these two eyes that block our channel to other dimensions. They function as a shield, so we can only see objects that exist in our physical dimension. Opening tianmu allows one to see without using these two eyes. After reaching a very high level, you can also cultivate to have a True Eye. Then you can see with the True Eye of Tianmu or the True Eye at the shangen point. According to the Buddha School, every pore is an eye—there are eyes all over the body. According to the Tao School, every acupuncture point is an eye. The main passage is nonetheless located at tianmu, and it must be opened first. In class, I plant in everyone things that can open tianmu. Owing to differences in people's physical quality, the results vary. Some people see a dark hole similar to a deep well; this means the passage of tianmu is dark. Others see a white tunnel. If objects can be seen in front, tianmu is about to open. Some see objects revolving; these are what Master[17] has planted to open tianmu. You will be able to see once tianmu is drilled open. Some people can see a large eye through their tianmu, and they think it is the Buddha's eye. In fact, it is their own eye. These are usually people with relatively good inborn quality.

According to our statistics, each time we give a lecture series, more than half of the attendees have their tianmu opened. A problem might arise after tianmu is opened, wherein a person whose xinxing isn't high can easily use tianmu to do bad things. To prevent this problem, I open your tianmu directly to the level of Wisdom Eyesight—in other words, to an advanced level that allows you to directly see scenes from other dimensions and to see things that appear during cultivation, making you believe them.

---

[17] Master—(also called Teacher) respectful way to address a teacher in China.

12

It will reinforce your confidence in cultivation. For people who have just started practicing, their xinxing have not yet reached the level of supernormal people. So once they possess supernormal things, they are inclined to do wrong. Let's give a playful example: If you walk along the street and come upon a lottery place, you might be able to walk away with first prize. This is to illustrate the point, and it is not allowed to happen. Another reason is that we are opening tianmu for a large number of people. Suppose everyone's tianmu were opened at a lower level: Just imagine that if everyone could see through the human body or see objects behind walls—could we still call this a human society? Human society would be severely disrupted, so it is neither permissible nor achievable. Furthermore, it wouldn't do practitioners any good, and it would only foster their attachments. Therefore, we won't open tianmu for you at a lower level. Instead, we will open it directly at a higher level.

(2) Tianmu's Levels

Tianmu has different levels. Corresponding to its level, it sees different dimensions. According to Buddhism there are five levels: the Flesh Eyesight, the Celestial Eyesight, the Wisdom Eyesight, the Law Eyesight, and the Buddha's Eyesight. Each level is subdivided into upper, middle and lower levels. At or below the level of the Celestial Eyesight, it can only observe our material world. Only at or above the Wisdom Eyesight level will it be able to observe other dimensions. Those who have the supernormal ability of penetrative sight can see things accurately, with clarity better than that of CT scanning. But what they can see is still within this physical world and doesn't exceed the dimension in which we exist; it's not considered to have reached the advanced level of tianmu.

Tianmu's level is determined by the amount of a person's quintessential qi, as well as the width, brightness, and degree of blockage of the main passage. The internal, quintessential qi is critical in determining how thoroughly tianmu can open. It is particularly easy to open tianmu for children under the age of six. I needn't even bother using my hand. It opens once I start talking, for children have received little negative influence from our physical world and they haven't committed any wrongdoing. Their quintessential qi is well preserved. As to children over the age of six, their tianmu become increasingly difficult to open, owing to the increase of external influences as they grow up. Particularly, unsound education, being spoiled, and turning immoral can all make the quintessential qi dissipate. After reaching a certain point, all of it will be gone. Those people whose quintessential qi is completely lost can gradually recover it through cultivation, but it takes a long period of time and arduous effort. The quintessential qi is thus extremely precious.

I don't recommend that people's tianmu be opened at the level of Celestial Eyesight, because when the cultivator's energy potency is low, he loses more energy looking at objects than he collects through cultivation. If too much of the essential energy is lost, tianmu may once again close. Once it closes, it won't be easy to open again. Therefore, when I open tianmu for people, I usually open it at the level of Wisdom Eyesight. No matter how clear or unclear their vision is, cultivators will be able to see objects in other dimensions. Affected by innate qualities, some people can see clearly, some see things intermittently, and others see unclearly. At minimum, however, you will be able to see light. This is beneficial to cultivators' progress toward higher levels. Those who can't see clearly will be able to remedy this through cultivation.

14

People who have less quintessential qi only see images in black and white through their tianmu. As to people who have relatively more quintessential qi, their tianmu will be able to see scenes in color and in a more clear form. The more the quintessential qi, the better the clarity. But each individual is different. Some people are born with tianmu open, while others' may be tightly clogged. When tianmu is opening, the image is similar to the blooming of a flower, opening layer after layer. During sitting meditation, initially you will discover illumination in the area of tianmu. At the beginning the illumination isn't so bright, while later it turns red. Some people's tianmu are very tightly closed, so their initial reactions may be quite strong. They will feel the muscles around the primary passage and the shangen point tightening, as if they were being pressed and squeezed inward. Their temples and forehead start to feel like they are swelling and aching, and these are all symptoms of tianmu opening. People whose tianmu open easily can occasionally see certain things. During my classes, there are people who unwittingly see my Law Bodies. When they intentionally try to look, it disappears, as they are then actually using their flesh eyes. When you see some things with eyes closed, try to remain in that state, and gradually you will see things more clearly. When you want to watch more closely, you will actually switch to your own eyes and use the optic nerves. You will then be unable to see anything.

The dimensions perceived by tianmu are different depending on the level of one's tianmu. Some scientific research departments fail to understand this principle, thus preventing some qigong experiments from reaching their expected outcomes. Occasionally, some experiments even reach opposite conclusions. For example, an institute designed a method to test supernormal abilities. They asked qigong masters to see the contents of a sealed box. Because of differences in the levels of their tianmu, not all of their answers were the same. The research staff thus regarded tianmu as false and a deceptive concept. People with tianmu at a lower level usually achieve better results with this kind of experiment, because their tianmu are opened at the level of the Celestial Eyesight—a level suitable only for observing objects in this physical dimension. So people who don't understand tianmu think that these people have the greatest supernormal abilities. All objects, organic or inorganic, appear in different shapes and forms in different dimensions. For example, as soon as a glass is manufactured, an intelligent being comes into existence in a different dimension. Moreover, prior to the existence of this being, it might have been something else. When tianmu is at the lowest level, one will see a glass. At a higher level, one will see the being that exists in the other dimension. At an even higher level, one will see the material form prior to the existence of that intelligent being.

(3) Remote Sight

After tianmu is opened, the supernormal ability of remote sight will emerge for some, and they will be able to see objects thousands of miles away. Each individual occupies some space of his own. In that space, he is as big as a universe. Within his particular space, he has a mirror in front of his forehead, but it is invisible in our dimension. Everyone has this mirror, but nonpractitioners' mirror faces inwards. For cultivators, this mirror gradually turns over. Once it turns over, this mirror can reflect what the cultivator wants to see. In his particular space he is rather large—his body is fairly large. So is his mirror. Whatever the cultivator wants to see can be reflected onto the mirror. But he still cannot see the image even though the mirror has captured it;

the image should remain on the mirror for a split second. The mirror will then turn back. After allowing you to see the objects it reflects, it will turn over again. It will flip back over very quickly, flipping back and forth ceaselessly. Films move at twenty-four frames per second to produce continuous movement. The speed at which the mirror flips is much faster than that, and so the images seem continuous and clear. This is remote sight—the principle of remote sight is this simple. This used to be very secretive, yet I have revealed it with just a few lines.

(4) Dimensions

From our perspective, dimensions are very complicated. Mankind only knows the dimension in which human beings currently exist, while other dimensions haven't yet been explored or detected. When it comes to other dimensions, we qigong masters have already seen dozens of levels of dimensions. These, too, can be explained theoretically, but they remain unproven by science. Certain things, even if you don't admit their existence, have actually reflected into our dimension. For example, there is a place called the Bermuda Triangle, a.k.a. "the devils triangle." Some ships have disappeared in that area, and some planes have also disappeared, reemerging years later. No one can explain why. No one has gone beyond the confines of human thoughts and theories. In fact, the Triangle is a passage to another dimension. Unlike our regular doors with definite positions, it remains in an unpredictable state. If the ship happens to enter when the door is coincidentally opened, it can easily go into the other dimension. Human beings cannot sense the differences between dimensions, and they enter into another dimension instantly. The time-space difference between that dimension and our dimension cannot be expressed in miles—a distance of thousands of miles might be contained in one point here, that is, they might exist in the same place and at the same time. The ship swings in for a moment and comes back out again by accident. Yet decades have passed in this world, because time is different in these two dimensions. In addition, there are unitary worlds existing in each dimension. Here, there is a similarity to our models of atomic structures wherein one ball is connected to another by a string, involving many balls and strings, which is very complex.

Four years prior to World War II, a British pilot was carrying out a mission. In the middle of his flight he ran into a heavy thunderstorm. Drawing upon his experiences, he was able to find an abandoned airport. The moment the airport appeared before his eyes, a completely different picture came into view: All of a sudden it was sunny and cloudless, as if he had just emerged from another world. The airplanes at the airport were already colored in yellow, while people were busy doing things on the ground. He felt very strange. After he touched down, no one acknowledged him; even the radar tower didn't contact him. The pilot decided to leave since the sky had cleared up. He flew again, and when he was at the same distance where he had seen the airport moments ago, he again plunged into the thunderstorm. He eventually managed to get back. He reported the situation, and even wrote it down in the flight record. But his superior didn't believe him. Four years later World War II broke out, and he was transferred to that abandoned airport. He immediately recalled that it was exactly the same scene he had seen four years before. All of us qigong masters know how to explain it. He did the identical thing four years in advance as he would do later. Before the first act had begun, he had gone there and played his role in advance, then returning to the right order.

18

5. Qigong Treatments and Hospital Treatments

Theoretically speaking, qigong treatments are completely different from the treatments given at hospitals. Western treatments utilize methods of ordinary human society. Despite means such as lab tests and X-ray examinations, they can only observe the sources of illness in this dimension, and they cannot see the information that exists in other dimensions. Therefore, they fail to understand the cause of the illness. If the patient isn't seriously ill, medication can remove or drive away the origin of the illness (which is considered a virus by Western doctors, and karmic debt in qigong). In the event where the illness is serious, medicine will be ineffective. If its dose is increased, a person might be unable to bear it. Not all diseases are constrained by the laws of this world and some diseases are very serious, exceeding the confines of this world, and as a result, hospitals are incapable of treating them.

Chinese Medicine is the traditional medical science in our country. It is inseparable from the supernormal abilities developed through human body cultivation. Ancient people paid special attention to cultivation of the human body. The Confucian School, the Tao School, the Buddha School, and even the students of Confucianism have all attached importance to meditation. Sitting meditation was considered a skill. Even though they didn't practice exercise, over the course of time they still developed energy potency and supernormal abilities. Why did Chinese acupuncture so clearly detect the meridians[18] in the human body? Why aren't the acupuncture points connected horizontally? Why aren't they crossed, and why are they connected vertically? Why were they mapped out with such accuracy? Modern people with supernormal abilities can see with their own eyes the same things that were

---

[18] meridian—energy channels in one's body.

portrayed by Chinese doctors. This is because ancient Chinese doctors generally had supernormal abilities. In Chinese history, Li Shizhen, Sun Simiao, Bian Que, and Hua Tuo[19] were all in fact qigong masters with supernormal abilities. In being passed down to this day, Chinese Medicine has lost the component that was connected to supernormal abilities and only retained the techniques of treatment. In the past, Chinese doctors used the eyes (with supernormal abilities) to diagnose disease. Later, they also developed the method of taking the pulse. If supernormal abilities were added back into the Chinese methods of treatment, one could say that Western Medicine wouldn't be able to catch up with Chinese doctors for many years to come.

Qigong treatment eliminates the root cause of an illness. I regard illness as one type of karma: Treating an illness is to help diminish karma. Some qigong masters treat disease by helping the patient discharge black qi, using the method of discharging and supplementing qi. At a very low level these masters discharge black qi, yet they don't know the root cause of the black qi. This black qi will return and the illness will relapse. The truth is that the black qi is not the cause of the illness—the existence of black qi only makes the patient feel uncomfortable. The root cause of his illness is an intelligent being that exists in another dimension. Many qigong masters don't know this. Since that intelligent being is very mighty, average people cannot touch it, and they do not dare. Treatment by Falun Gong focuses on and starts with that intelligent being, removing the root cause of the illness. Moreover, a shield is installed in that area so that the illness will be unable to invade again in the future.

---

[19] Li Shizhen (lee shr-jhun), Sun Simiao (sun szz-meow), Bian Que (byen chueh), and Huatuo (hwa-twoah)—well-known doctors of Chinese medicine in history.

Qigong can heal diseases but it cannot interfere with the condition of human society. If applied on a large scale, it would interfere with the condition of ordinary human society, which is not allowed; neither would its healing effects be good. As all of you know, some people have opened qigong diagnostic clinics, qigong hospitals, and qigong recovery centers. Before they opened these businesses, their treatments' efficacy might have been good. Once they opened a business to treat illness, the effectiveness plummeted. This means people are prohibited from using supernatural laws to fulfill the functions of ordinary human society. Doing so certainly reduces its effectiveness to a level as low as the principle of ordinary human society.

Using supernormal abilities, one can observe the inside of a human body layer by layer, as in medical sectioning. Soft tissues and any other part of the body can be seen. Though the current CT scan is able to see very clearly, a machine still has to be used; it is very time consuming, uses a great deal of film, is very slow and costly. It's not as convenient or accurate as human supernormal abilities. By closing their eyes to do a quick browse, qigong masters are able to see directly and clearly any part of the patient. Isn't this high tech? This high technology is even more advanced than modern high technology. Yet this kind of skill already existed in ancient China—it was the high technology of ancient times. Hua Tuo discovered a tumor growing in the brain of Cao Cao[20] and wanted to perform surgery on him. Cao Cao couldn't accept it and mistook it as a way to harm him. He had Hua Tuo arrested. In the end, Cao Cao consequently died of the brain tumor. Many well-known Chinese doctors in history actually possessed supernormal abilities. It is just that people in this modern society

---

[20] Cao Cao (tsaow-tsaow)—emperor of one of the three kingdoms (220 A.D.-265 A.D.).

zealously pursue practical things and have forgotten the ancient traditions.

Our high-level qigong cultivation is to reexamine traditional things, inherit and develop them through practice, and reuse them to benefit human society.

6. Qigong of the Buddha School and Buddhism

The moment we mention qigong of the Buddha School, many people think of an issue: Since the goal of the Buddha School is to cultivate Buddhahood, they start to relate it to the things of Buddhism. I hereby solemnly clarify that Falun Gong is qigong of the Buddha School. It is a righteous, great cultivation way, and has nothing to do with Buddhism. Qigong of the Buddha School is qigong of the Buddha School, while Buddhism is Buddhism. Although they have the same goal in cultivation, they take different paths. They are different schools of practice with different requirements. I mentioned the word "Buddha," and I will mention it again later when I explain gong at higher levels. The word itself doesn't embody any superstitious connotations. Some people turn crazy when they hear the word Buddha, claiming that we propagate superstition. It is not so. "Buddha" was originally a Sanskrit term, originating in India. Translated according to its pronunciation, it was called "Fo Tuo"[21] [in China]. People omitted the "Tuo," keeping the word "Fo." Translated into Chinese, it means "the enlightened," a person who is enlightened. (Refer to the Ci Hai[22] dictionary.)

---

[21] Fo Tuo (foah-toah)—Buddha.

[22] Ci Hai (tsz hi)—the name of a Chinese dictionary.

(1) Qigong of the Buddha School

At present, two types of Buddha School qigong have been made public. One separated from Buddhism, and it has produced many distinguished monks throughout its thousands of years of development. When they have cultivated to a very advanced level during their cultivation, a high-level master teaches them so that they can receive personal teachings from a higher level. In the past, all of these things in Buddhism used to be passed down to one individual at a time. Only when he was near the end of his life would the distinguished monk pass these down to one disciple who would cultivate according to Buddhist doctrines, improving holistically. This type of qigong seems closely connected to Buddhism. Monks were driven out of the temples later, namely, during the period of "the Great Cultural Revolution."[23] These exercises spread to the general public, where they developed greatly in number.

Another type of qigong is also of the Buddha School. Throughout history, this type has never been a part of Buddhism. It has always been practiced quietly, either among the populace or deep in the mountains. These practices all have their uniqueness. They require choosing a good disciple—someone with tremendous de who is truly capable of cultivating toward an advanced level. This kind of person appears in this world only once in many, many years. These practices cannot be made public. They require very high xinxing, and their gong develops very rapidly. These kinds of practices are not few. It is the same with the Tao School. Taoist qigong, while all belonging to the Tao School, are further divided into Kunlun, Emei, Wudang, etc. There are different subdivisions within each division, and the

---

[23] "Great Cultural Revolution"—a communist political movement that denounced traditional values and culture (1966-1976).

subdivisions are very different from one another. They cannot be mixed and practiced together.

(2) Buddhism

Buddhism is a system of cultivation practice enlightened to by Sakyamuni himself in India more than two thousand years ago, based on his original cultivation practice. It can be summarized in three words: precept, samadhi,[24] wisdom. "Precept" is for the purpose of samadhi. Though Buddhism doesn't discuss exercises, it does in fact have exercises. Buddhists are indeed practicing exercise when they sit down and enter a tranquil state. This is because when a person calms down and settles his mind, energy from the cosmos starts to gather about his body, achieving the effect of practicing. The precepts in Buddhism are for abandoning all human desires and relinquishing everything to which an everyday person is attached. Consequently, the monk can reach the state of peacefulness and stillness, enabling him to enter samadhi. A person continuously improves himself in samadhi, eventually becoming an enlightened person and obtaining wisdom. He will then know the universe and see the truth of the universe.

During his teaching of the Dharma, Sakyamuni did only three things daily: teaching Dharma (primarily Dharma of Arhat) to his disciples, carrying a bowl to collect alms (begging for food), and cultivating through sitting in meditation. After Sakyamuni left this world, Brahmanism and Buddhism battled. Afterwards, these two religions merged into one, called Hinduism. Thus, Buddhism no longer exists in India today. With later developments and evolutions, Mahayana[25] Buddhism appeared and was spread to inland China, becoming today's [Chinese] Buddhism.

[24] Samadhi—in Buddhism, "meditation in trance."
[25] Mahayana—"the Great Vehicle Buddhism."

24

Mahayana Buddhism doesn't worship Sakyamuni as its sole progenitor—it is a multi-Buddha faith. It believes in many Tathagatas, such as Buddha Amitabha, Medicine Buddha, etc. There are more precepts, and the goal of cultivation has become higher. Back then, Sakyamuni taught the Dharma of Bodhisattva to a few disciples. These teachings were later reorganized and have developed into today's Mahayana Buddhism, which is for cultivating to the realm of Bodhisattva. To this day in Southeast Asia, the tradition of Hinayana[26] Buddhism has been retained, and ceremonies are executed using supernormal abilities. In Buddhism's course of evolution, one school branched off to the Tibet region of our country and is called Tibetan Tantrism. Another school spread to the *Han*[27] area via Xinjiang[28] and was called Tang Tantrism (this disappeared after Buddhism was suppressed during the years of Huichang[29]). Another branch in India evolved into yoga.

In Buddhism there is no teaching of exercises, and neither is qigong practiced. This is to preserve the traditional way of Buddhist cultivation. It is also an important reason why Buddhism has lasted more than two thousand years without waning. It is precisely because it didn't accept anything foreign to it that it has naturally maintained its own tradition. There are different ways to cultivate in Buddhism. Hinayana Buddhism focuses on self-salvation and self-cultivation; Mahayana Buddhism has already developed into salvation of both self and others—salvation of all sentient beings.

---

[26] Hinayana—"the Small Vehicle Buddhism."

[27] *Han* (hahn)—the majority ethnicity of Chinese people.

[28] Xinjiang (shin-jyang)—a province in Northwestern China.

[29] Huichang (hway chahng)—Emperor Wu Zong's time of Tang Dynasty (841 A.D.-846 A.D.).

7. Righteous Cultivation Ways and Evil Ways

(1) The Side-Door Clumsy Way *(Pangmen Zuodao)*

The Side-Door Clumsy Way is also called the *Qimen*[30] cultivation practice. There were various qigong cultivation ways existing prior to the establishment of religions. There are many practices outside of religion that have spread among the populace. Lacking systematic theories, most of them haven't become complete cultivation systems. Nonetheless, the Qimen cultivation practice has its own systematic, complete, and unusually intense cultivation method, and it, too, has been spread among the populace. These exercises are frequently called Side-Door Clumsy Way. Why are they called this? Literally, "Pangmen" means "side door"; "Zuodao" means "clumsy way." People consider both the Buddha School and the Tao School ways of cultivation to be straight, with all others being Side-Door Clumsy Ways, or evil cultivation ways. Actually, it's not so. The Side-Door Clumsy Way has been practiced secretly throughout history, and it has been taught to one disciple at a time. It's not allowed to be revealed to the public. Once it is out, people will not understand it very well. Even the practitioners proclaim that it is of neither the Buddha School nor the Tao School. Its cultivation principles have strict requirements for xinxing. It cultivates according to the characteristics of the universe, advocating doing kind deeds and guarding xinxing. The highly-accomplished masters in this school all have unique skills, and some of their unique techniques are powerful. I have met three highly-accomplished masters from the Qimen cultivation practice who taught me some things that cannot be found in either the Buddha or Tao Schools. These things were each fairly difficult to practice during the process of cultivation, so the cultivated

---

[30] *Qimen* (chee-mun) —"unconventional School."

gong was very unique. Contrarily, among some so-called Buddha and Tao Schools of cultivation, strict xinxing requirements are lacking and their practitioners thus cannot cultivate to an advanced level. We therefore should look at each cultivation school objectively.

(2) Martial Arts Qigong

Martial arts qigong is born of a long history. With its own complete system of theories and cultivation methods, it has formed an independent system. Yet strictly speaking, it only manifests supernormal abilities that are generated by internal cultivation at the lowest level. All the supernormal abilities that appear in martial arts cultivation appear in internal cultivation as well. Martial arts cultivation also begins with practicing qi. For instance, when striking a piece of rock, in the beginning [the martial arts practitioner] needs to swing his arms to transport qi. Over time, his qi will change in nature and become an energy mass that appears to exist in the form of light. Upon reaching this stage, gong will start to function. Because gong is evolved matter, it is intelligent. It exists in another dimension and is controlled by the thoughts coming from the brain. When attacked, [the martial arts practitioner] doesn't need to transport qi; gong will come merely with a thought. Over the course of cultivation, his gong will continually be strengthened, with its particles turning finer and its energy growing greater. The skills of "iron sand palm" and "cinnabar palm" will appear. In movies, magazines, and on television in recent years, the skills of "golden bell shield" and "iron cloth shirt" have emerged. These stem from the simultaneous practice of internal cultivation and martial arts cultivation. They come from cultivating the internal and external at the same time. To cultivate internally, a person needs to value de and cultivate his xinxing. Theoretically speaking, when his ability reaches a certain level, it will make gong emit from the interior to the exterior of the body. Because of its high density, it becomes a protective shield. In terms of principles, the biggest difference between the martial arts and our internal cultivation lies in the fact that the martial arts are practiced with vigorous movements and do not enter into tranquility. Not being tranquil makes qi flow underneath the skin and pass through the muscles, instead of flowing into *dantian*.[31] So they don't cultivate life, and neither are they able to.

(3) Reverse Cultivation and Energy Borrowing

Some people have never practiced qigong. Then suddenly they acquire gong overnight, with quite strong energy. Moreover, they are able to heal disease for others. People call them qigong masters and they are teaching others as well. Some of them, despite the fact that they have never learned qigong or have only learned a few of its movements, are teaching people things that they have modified slightly. This kind of person isn't qualified to be a qigong master. He doesn't have anything to pass on to others. What he teaches certainly cannot be used to cultivate toward a high level; at most, it can help get rid of sickness and improve health. How does this kind of gong come about? Let's first talk about reverse cultivation. The commonly-known phrase "reverse cultivation" pertains to those good people who have extremely high xinxing. They are usually older, such as above fifty years of age. Time is insufficient for them to cultivate from the beginning, as it's not easy to meet excellent masters who teach [qigong] exercises that cultivate both mind and body. The moment that such a person

---

[31] *dantian* (dahn-tyen)—"field of dan"; the lower abdominal area.

28

wants to cultivate, high-level masters will load a great amount of energy onto him according to his xinxing foundation, enabling him to cultivate in reverse, from the top down. This way it is much faster. High-level masters perform the transformation in the air, continuously adding energy to the person from outside of his body; this is particularly so when the person is giving treatments and forming an energy field. The energy given by the masters flows as if through a pipeline. Some people don't even know where the energy comes from. This is reverse cultivation.

Another matter is called "energy borrowing," and this isn't restricted in terms of age. Besides the main consciousness, a human being also has an assistant consciousness(es) that is generally at a higher level than the main consciousness. Some people's assistant consciousness(es) have reached such high levels that they can communicate with enlightened beings. When these kinds of people want to cultivate, their assistant consciousness(es) also wants to improve its level. It immediately gets in touch with those enlightened beings and borrows energy from them. After being loaned energy, such a person will get gong overnight. After attaining gong, he will be able to treat people to ease their pain. He usually adopts the method of forming an energy field. Additionally, he will be able to give energy out individually to people and teach some techniques.

People like that usually start out pretty well. Possessing gong and becoming well-known, they acquire both fame and personal gain. Fame and personal gain come to occupy a substantial portion of their thinking—more than that of cultivation. From that point on, their gong starts to drop, becoming smaller and smaller until finally it is all gone.

(4) Cosmic Language

Some people suddenly speak a certain type of language. It sounds fairly fluent when uttered; yet it's not a language of any human society. What is it called? It is called the cosmic language. The so-called cosmic language is in fact merely a language of those beings who are not so high. At present, around the country this phenomenon is occurring for quite a few qigong practitioners; some of them can even speak several different languages. Of course, the languages of our humankind are very sophisticated, with more than a thousand varieties. Is the cosmic language considered a supernormal ability? I say that it doesn't count as one. It's not a supernormal ability that comes from you, neither is it a kind of capability that is given to you from the outside. Rather, it is manipulation by foreign beings. These beings originate at a somewhat higher level—at least higher than that of humankind. It is one of them who does the talking; the person who speaks a cosmic language only serves as a median. Most people don't even know themselves what they are saying. Only those who have mind-reading capabilities can get a general sense for what the words mean. It's not supernormal ability, but many people who have spoken the language feel superior and complacent since they think it is a supernormal ability. In fact, people with tianmu at a high level can definitely observe that a living being is speaking from diagonally above, through the person's mouth.

That being teaches the person the cosmic language while passing on to him some of its gong. Yet thereafter this person will be in its control. Therefore, this is not a righteous way. Even though it is in a slightly higher dimension, that being isn't cultivating a righteous way. It therefore doesn't know how to teach cultivators to keep fit or heal disease. Consequently, it utilizes this method of sending out energy through speech. Since

30

this energy is dispersed, it has very little power. It is effective in treating minor sickness, but fails with serious illness. Buddhism speaks of how people above lack suffering and conflict, and how they therefore cannot cultivate; furthermore, they cannot temper themselves and are unable to improve their levels. They thus look for ways to help people gain better health, thereby improving themselves. This is what the cosmic language is all about. The cosmic language is not a supernormal ability, and neither is it qigong.

(5) Spirit Possession

The most injurious type of spirit possession is possession by a low-level being; this is caused by cultivating an evil way. It is very harmful to people, and the consequences of people being possessed are frightening. Not long after practicing, some people become obsessed with becoming rich; they think of these things all the time. Originally, these people might have been pretty decent or might have already had a master looking after them. Nevertheless, things turn sour when they start to contemplate giving treatments and getting rich. They then attract this type of being. It is not in our material dimension, and yet it truly exists.

Such a practitioner suddenly feels that his tianmu is open and that he now has gong, but it is actually the possessing spirit that has control of his brain. It reflects the images that it sees onto the person's brain, making him feel that his tianmu has been opened. Actually, his tianmu has not been opened whatsoever. Why does the possessing spirit want to give him gong? Why does it want to help him? It is because animals are forbidden to cultivate in our universe. Since animals know nothing about xinxing and cannot improve themselves, they are not allowed to obtain the righteous way. As a result, they want to attach themselves to human bodies and acquire the human essence. There is also another rule in this universe, namely: no loss, no gain. They thus want to satisfy your desire for fame and personal gain. They make you rich and famous, but they don't help you for nothing. They also want to gain something—your essence. When they leave you, you will have nothing left and turn very weak or become a vegetable. This is caused by a crooked xinxing. One right mind will subdue a hundred evils. When you are righteous, you will not attract evil. In other words, be a noble practitioner, turn away from all nonsense, and only cultivate the righteous way.

(6) An Evil Way can be Produced in Righteous Practice

Although the gong learned by some people comes from righteous cultivation ways, people can actually inadvertently practice evil ways since they are unable to impose strict self-requirements, fail to cultivate xinxing, and entertain negative thoughts during practice. For example, when a person is practicing there, either in the standing stance or the sitting exercise, his thoughts are actually on money and personal gain, "He's wronged me, and I'll fix him after I acquire supernormal abilities." Or he is thinking of this or that supernormal ability, adding something very bad to his gong and actually practicing an evil way. This is very dangerous, as it may attract some very negative things, such as low-level beings. Perhaps the person doesn't even know he has invited them. Because his attachment is strong—purposefully practicing cultivation to fulfill desires is unacceptable—he isn't righteous, and even his master will be unable to protect him. Therefore, practitioners must maintain their xinxing strictly, keeping a righteous mind and craving nothing. Otherwise, problems might arise.

Chapter II
Falun Gong

Falun Gong originates from Falun Xiulian[32] Dafa in the Buddha School. It is a special cultivation way of Buddha School qigong. Yet it has its own distinctive qualities that set it apart from average ways of cultivation in the Buddha School. This cultivation system is a special, intense cultivation method that used to require cultivators to have extremely high xinxing and great inborn quality. In order to have more practitioners improve while also satisfying the needs of a massive number of dedicated cultivators, I have redesigned and made public this set of cultivation methods that are suitable for popularization. In spite of the modifications, this practice still far exceeds the teachings and levels in other practices.

1. Falun's Function

The Falun of Falun Gong retains the same characteristics as the universe, as it is a miniature of the universe. Cultivators of Falun Gong will not only rapidly develop supernormal abilities and energy potency, they will also develop an incomparably powerful Falun in a very short period of time. Once fully developed, Falun exists as an intelligent being. It automatically spins ceaselessly in the practitioner's lower abdominal area, constantly absorbing and transforming energy from the universe, and ultimately converting it in the practitioner's benti to gong. Consequently,

---

[32] Xiulian (shyo-lyen)—cultivation practice.

the effect of "the Fa refines the practitioner" is achieved. This means that although this person doesn't practice every minute, Falun constantly refines him. Internally, Falun offers salvation to oneself. It makes the person stronger and healthier, more intelligent and wise, and it protects the practitioner from deviation. It can also protect the cultivator from interference from people with inferior xinxing. Externally, Falun can heal sickness and eliminate evil for others, rectifying all abnormal conditions. Falun rotates continuously in the lower abdominal area, clockwise nine times and then counterclockwise nine times. When rotating clockwise, it vigorously absorbs energy from the universe; the energy is very strong. As one's energy potency progresses, its rotational power becomes stronger. This is a state that cannot be attained by deliberate attempts to pour qi into the top of the head. When rotating counterclockwise, it releases energy and provides salvation to all beings, rectifying abnormal states. People around the practitioner benefit. Of all the qigong practices taught in our country, Falun Gong is the first and only cultivation method that has achieved "the Fa refines the practitioner."

Falun is most precious and cannot be exchanged for any amount of money. When passing Falun on to me, my master told me that Falun shouldn't be passed on to anyone else; all of those people who have cultivated for thousands of years want to have it, yet they cannot. This school of cultivation can only be passed on to one person after a very, very long time, unlike those that are passed on to one person every few decades. Falun is therefore extremely precious. Even though we have now made it public and altered it to become less powerful, it is still extremely precious. As to cultivators who have acquired it, they are halfway through their cultivation. What remains is only for you to upgrade your xinxing, and a fairly advanced level awaits you. Of course, people who are not predestined may later stop after cultivating for a little while, and then the Falun in them will cease to exist.

Falun Gong is of the Buddha School, but it far exceeds the scope of the Buddha School: It cultivates the entire universe. In the past, cultivation in the Buddha School only talked about principles of the Buddha School, while cultivation in the Tao School only addressed principles of the Tao School. Neither thoroughly explained the universe at the fundamental level. The universe is similar to human beings, in that aside from its material composition, it also has its own characteristics. They can be summarized in three words: Zhen, Shan, and Ren. Tao School cultivation focuses its understanding on Zhen—telling the truth, doing honest deeds, returning to the original, true self, and finally becoming a "true person." Buddha School cultivation focuses on Shan—developing great compassion and offering salvation to all beings. Our cultivation way cultivates Zhen, Shan, and Ren simultaneously, directly cultivating in accordance with the fundamental characteristics of the universe, and eventually assimilating one to the universe.

Falun Gong cultivates both mind and body. When one's energy potency and xinxing have reached a certain level, as a requirement [of our school], one is to reach the state of enlightenment (the final release of gong) in this world and attain an indestructible body. In general, Falun Gong is divided into In-Triple-World-Law, Beyond-Triple-World-Law, and many other levels. I hope that all devoted practitioners will cultivate diligently and continually improve their xinxing, so that they can reach enlightenment and attain completion of cultivation *(yuanman)*.

2. Falun's Configuration

The Falun of Falun Gong is an intelligent, spinning body of high-energy substance. It rotates according to the order of the entire celestial cosmos' movement. To a certain extent, Falun is a miniature of the universe.

In the center of Falun there is a Buddha School symbol of *srivatsa*, "卍", (in Sanskrit, srivatsa means "the gathering of all good fortune" (refer to the Ci Hai dictionary)), which is the core of Falun. Its color is close to golden yellow, while the base color is bright red. The base color of the outer ring is orange. Four symbols of *taiji*[33] and four Buddha School *srivatsa* are arranged alternately in eight directions. The taiji that consist of red and black colors belong to the Tao School, while the taiji consisting of red and blue are of the Great Primordial-Tao School. The four small *srivatsa* are also golden yellow. The base color of Falun changes periodically between red, orange, yellow, green, blue, indigo, and violet. These are very beautiful colors (refer to the color insert). The colors of the central *srivatsa*, "卍", and the taiji do not change. These Falun of different sizes rotate on their own, as does the *srivatsa*, "卍". Falun's root is planted in the universe. The universe is rotating, all galaxies are rotating, and thus, Falun is also rotating. Those whose tianmu are at a lower level can see Falun spinning like a fan; those whose tianmu are at a higher level can see the whole image of Falun, which is very beautiful and brilliant, and this encourages practitioners to strive forward vigorously.

---

[33] *taiji* (tie-jee)—the symbol of the Tao School.

3. Characteristics of Falun Gong Cultivation

(1) The Fa Refines the Practitioner

People who study Falun Gong can not only rapidly develop their energy potency and supernormal abilities, but also procure a Falun through cultivation. Falun can form in a very short period of time, and once formed, it is very powerful. It can protect practitioners from deviating. Additionally, it can protect the person against interference from people with inferior xinxing. In terms of its theories, Falun Gong is totally different from traditional cultivation methods. Since, after forming, Falun ceaselessly rotates on its own, it exists in the form of an intelligent being, regularly and continuously collecting energy in the practitioner's lower abdominal area. Falun automatically absorbs energy from the universe by rotating. Precisely because it rotates incessantly, it reaches the goal of "the Fa refines the practitioner"; this refers to the fact that Falun cultivates people ceaselessly, even though people don't practice all the time. As everyone knows, everyday people have to work during the day and rest at night, leaving very limited time for practice. In order to achieve continuous practice twenty-four hours a day, the way called "thinking about practice all the time" is unsuitable, and using other methods still hardly achieves the goal of twenty-four hours of cultivation in the true sense. Yet Falun rotates ceaselessly, and when rotating inward it absorbs a great amount of qi (the initial form of energy's existence). Day and night, Falun keeps storing and transforming the absorbed qi in each and every location of Falun. It converts qi into a substance of a higher level, ultimately turning it—in the cultivator's body—into gong. This is "the Fa refines the practitioner." Falun Gong's cultivation is entirely different from all other schools or qigong cultivation methods that cultivate dan.

The biggest feature of Falun Gong is the cultivation of Falun rather than dan. Until now, among the cultivation methods that have been made public, regardless of which school or cultivation way they come from—be they branches of Buddhism or Taoism, of the Buddha or Tao School, or of the branches spread among people—all of them cultivate dan. So do many side-door cultivation ways. They are called the "dan way of qigong."[34] The cultivation used by monks, nuns and Taoists have taken this path of cultivating dan. If cremated upon death, such persons will produce sarira,[35] the composition of which has not been discerned by modern scientific equipment. The sarira are very solid, firm and beautiful. Actually, they are a high-energy substance that was gathered from other dimensions—not our dimension. That is dan. It is very difficult for those who practice the dan way of qigong to reach the state of enlightenment during one's lifetime. In the past, a lot of people who practiced the dan way of qigong tried to lift their dan. Once lifted to the *niwan* palace,[36] it couldn't be lifted out, and so these people got stuck here. Some people wanted to deliberately burst it, but had no way of doing so. There were some cases like this: a person's grandfather didn't succeed in cultivation, so at the end of his lifetime he spat it out and passed it on to his father; his father didn't succeed in cultivation, so at the end of his lifetime he spat it out and passed it on to this person. To this day, he still has not achieved much. It's very difficult! Of course, there are many decent cultivation methods. It is not so bad if you can receive genuine teaching from someone, but chances are he won't teach you high-level things.

---

[34] Qigong systems that cultivate Dan.

[35] sarira—the special remains consisting of dan left behind after a monk is cremated.

[36] *niwan* (nee-wahn) palace—Taoist term for pineal body.

(2) Cultivation of Main Consciousness

Everyone has a main consciousness. One usually relies on one's main consciousness to act and think. Besides the main consciousness, there also exists in the body one or more assistant consciousnesses and inherited messages from one's ancestors. The assistant consciousness(es) has the same name as the main consciousness, but in general it is more capable and of a higher level. It does not get lost in the maze of our human society and can see its particular dimension. Many cultivation methods take the route of cultivating the assistant consciousness(es), whereby one's physical body and main consciousness only function as a vehicle. Generally, practitioners don't know about these things, and they even feel very good about themselves. It is incredibly difficult for one to give up practical things while living in society, particularly those things that one is attached to. Therefore, many cultivation methods emphasize practicing while in the state of trance—an absolute state of trance. When transformation occurs during the state of trance, the assistant consciousness(es), in fact, gets transformed in a different society and improved in this process. One day, the assistant consciousness(es) completes its cultivation and takes away your gong. Nothing is left for your main consciousness and benti, and your lifelong cultivation falls short of success. That is a great pity. Some well-known qigong masters command great supernormal abilities of all kinds, and along with these, reputation and respect; however, they still don't know that their gong has not actually grown on their own bodies.

Our Falun Gong directly cultivates the main consciousness; we require that gong actually grows on your body. Of course, the assistant consciousness will also get a share, because being in a secondary position it also improves. Our cultivation method has a strict xinxing requirement, letting you temper your xinxing and gain improvement while in human society, under the most complicated circumstances—like a lotus flower emerging out of dirty mud. You are thus allowed to succeed in your cultivation. This is why Falun Gong is so precious: It is precious because it is you, yourself who attains the gong. But it is also very difficult. The difficulty lies in the fact that you have chosen a path on which you will be tempered and tested in the most complicated environment.

Since the goal of practice is to cultivate the main consciousness, the main consciousness must always be used to direct one's cultivation. The main consciousness should make the decision, rather than turning it over to the assistant consciousness(es). Otherwise, there will come a day when the assistant consciousness(es) will complete its cultivation at a higher level and take the gong with it. As the main body and main consciousness, you would have nothing left. As you are cultivating toward a higher level, it's not permissible to have your main consciousness be unaware that you are practicing, as if it were asleep. You must be clear that you are practicing, cultivating toward a higher level and improving your xinxing—only then will you be in control and able to acquire gong. Occasionally when you are absent-minded, you accomplish something without even knowing how it was done. It is actually the assistant consciousness(es) that is in effect; the assistant consciousness(es) is in command. If while sitting there in meditation you open your eyes to look across and you see that there is another you across the way, then that is your assistant consciousness(es). If you are sitting there in meditation facing north, but all of a sudden, you find that you are sitting on the north side, wondering, "How did I get out?", then this is your true self that has come out. What sits there is your physical body and assistant consciousness. These can be differentiated.

40

You shouldn't become completely unaware of yourself when practicing Falun Gong. Doing so isn't in line with the Great Way of Falun Gong cultivation. You must keep your mind clear when practicing. Deviation won't occur during practice if your main consciousness is strong, as nothing will really be able to harm you. If the main consciousness is weak, some things may come onto the body.

(3) Cultivate Regardless of Direction and Time

Many cultivation methods are particular about the direction toward which and the time when the practice is best done. We are not concerned with these in the least. Falun Gong cultivation is practiced according to the characteristics of the universe and the principles of the universe's evolution. Direction and time therefore are not important. We are, in effect, practicing while sitting on the Falun, which is all-directional and always rotating. Our Falun is synchronized with the universe. The universe is in motion, the Milky Way is in motion, the nine planets are revolving around the sun, and Earth itself is rotating. Which way is north, east, south or west? These directions were devised by people living on the earth. So whichever direction you face, you will be facing all directions.

Some people say it is best to practice at midnight, while some say at noon or some other time. We are not concerned about this, either, because Falun cultivates you when you are not practicing. Every moment Falun is helping you cultivate, which is "the Fa refines the practitioner." In the dan way of qigong, people cultivate dan; in Falun Gong, it is the Fa that cultivates people. Practice more when you have time, and practice less when you do not. It is quite flexible.

4. Cultivation of Both Mind and Body

Falun Gong cultivates both mind and body. Through practice, benti is changed first. Without losing benti, the main consciousness merges into one with the physical body, achieving complete cultivation of the entire being.

(1) Changing Benti

A human body is composed of flesh, blood, and bones, with different molecular structures and components. Through cultivation, the molecular composition of the human body is transformed into a substance of high energy. Thus, the human body is no longer composed of its original substance, and the human body has undergone a change in its fundamental nature. But cultivators cultivate and live among everyday people, and they cannot violate the conditions of human society. So this kind of change alters neither the body's original molecular structure, nor the sequence in which its molecules are arranged; it just changes the original molecular composition. The body's flesh remains soft, the bones are still hard and the blood is still fluid. When cut with a knife, one still bleeds. According to the Chinese Theory of the Five Elements, everything is composed of metal, wood, water, fire, and earth. It is the same with the human body. When a cultivator has undergone the changes in his benti whereby high-energy substances replace the original molecular components, the human body at that point is no longer composed of its original substances. This is the principle behind what is known as "transcending the five elements."

The most noticeable feature of cultivation methods that cultivate both mind and body is that they prolong life and deter aging. Our Falun Gong also has this noticeable feature. Falun Gong works this way: it fundamentally changes the molecular composition of the human body, storing in each cell the high-energy matter that has been gathered and ultimately allowing this high-energy matter to replace the cellular components. Metabolism no longer occurs. A person thus transcends the five elements, turning his body into one composed of substances from other dimensions. No longer restrained by our space and time, this person will forever be young.

There have been many accomplished monks in history who have had very long life spans. Now there are people who are hundreds of years old walking on the streets, and you cannot tell who they are. Looking very young, they wear the same clothes as everyday people, so you cannot distinguish them. The human life span shouldn't be as short as it is now. Speaking from the perspective of modern science, people should be able to live over two hundred years. According to the records, there was a person in Britain called Femcath who lived for 207 years. A person in Japan named Mitsu Taira lived to be 242 years old. During the Tang Dynasty in our country, there was a monk called Hui Zhao who lived to be 290 years old. According to the county annals of Yong Tai in Fujian Province, Chen Jun was born in the first year of Zhong He time (881 AD) under the reign of Emperor Xi Zong during the Tang Dynasty. He died in the Tai Ding time of the Yuan Dynasty (1324 AD), after living for 443 years. These are all backed up by records and can be investigated—they are not fairy tales. Through cultivation, our Falun Gong practitioners have come to have noticeably fewer wrinkles on their faces, which now have a rosy, healthy glow. Their bodies feel very light and relaxed, and they are not a bit tired when walking or working. This is a common phenomenon. I, myself, have cultivated for decades and others say that my face has not changed much in twenty years. This is the reason. Our Falun Gong contains very powerful things for cultivating the body. Falun Gong cultivators look very different in age from everyday people. They do not look their actual age. Therefore, the biggest features of cultivation methods that cultivate both mind and body are: prolonging life, deterring aging, and lengthening people's life expectancy.

(2) The Falun Heavenly Circuit

Our human body is a small universe. The energy of the human body circles around the body, and this is called "the circulation of the small universe," or "the heavenly circulation." Speaking in terms of levels, connecting the two energy meridians of *ren* and *du* is only a skin-deep heavenly circuit. It doesn't have the effect of cultivating the body. The Small Heavenly Circuit in the true sense goes from the niwan palace to dantian, circulating inside the body. Through the internal circulation, all meridians are opened up, expanding from the inside of the body to its outside. Our Falun Gong requires all meridians to be opened at the outset.

The Great Heavenly Circuit is the movement of the Rare Channels and Eight Meridians, and it goes around the entire body to complete one cycle. If the Great Heavenly Circuit is opened up, it will bring about a state in which a person can levitate off the ground. This is what is meant by "ascending in broad daylight", as written in Dan Jing. Nevertheless, a spot in your body will usually be locked so that you will be unable to fly. Yet it will bring you this state: You will walk quickly and effortlessly, and when you walk uphill you will feel as if someone were pushing you from behind. The opening of the Great Heavenly Circuit can also bring about a type of supernormal ability: It can make possible the exchange of the qi that exists in different organs of the body.

44

The qi of the heart will move to the stomach, the qi of the stomach will travel to the intestines, and so on. As one's energy potency strengthens, this capability will, if released outside the human body, become the supernormal ability of teleportation. This kind of heavenly circuit is also called "Meridian Heavenly Circuit," or "Qiankun Heavenly Circuit." Yet its movements still haven't achieved the goal of transforming the body. There has to be another corresponding heavenly circuit, called "Maoyou Heavenly Circuit." Here is how Maoyou Heavenly Circuit moves: It comes out from either the *huiyin* point[37] or the *baihui* point,[38] and moves along the sides of the body, where *yin* borders *yang*.[39]

The heavenly circuit in Falun Gong is much greater than the movements of the Rare Channels and Eight Meridians that are discussed in regular cultivation methods. It is the movement of all the criss-crossing meridians located throughout the entire body. It requires that all meridians of the entire body be thoroughly opened at once, and they must all move together. These things are already embedded in our Falun Gong, so you don't need to deliberately practice them, and neither should you guide them with your thoughts. If you do it that way, you will go awry. I install energy mechanisms *(qiji)* outside your body during the class, and they circulate automatically. The energy mechanism are something unique to cultivation at higher levels, and they are part of what makes our practice automatic. Just like Falun, they

---

[37] *huiyin* (hway-yeen) point—An acupuncture point in the center of the perineum.

[38] *baihui* (buy-hway) point—acupuncture point located at the crown of one's head.

[39] *yin* (yeen) and *yang* (yahng)—The Tao School believes that everything contains opposite forces of yin and yang which are mutually exclusive, yet interdependent, e.g. female (yin) vs. male (yang).

revolve ceaselessly, leading all internal energy meridians into a rotating motion. Even if you haven't practiced with the heavenly circuit, those energy meridians have, in fact, already been driven into motion, and deep inside and outside they are all moving together. We use our exercises to strengthen the energy mechanisms that exist outside the body.

(3) Opening the Meridians

The objective of opening the meridians is to allow energy to circulate and to change the molecular composition of cells, transforming them into a high-energy substance. The meridians of nonpractitioners are clogged and very narrow. The meridians of practitioners will gradually brighten, clearing out their clogged areas. The meridians of veteran practitioners will widen, and they will widen even further when cultivating at higher levels. Some people have meridians as wide as a finger. Yet the opening of meridians itself reflects neither one's cultivation level, nor the height of one's gong. Through practice, the meridians will be brightened and widened, eventually connecting to become one large piece. At that point, this person will have no meridians or acupuncture points. Conversely, his entire body will be meridians and acupuncture points. Even this stage doesn't mean that this person has attained the Tao. It is only one level's reflection during the process of Falun Gong cultivation. Upon arriving at this stage, this person has reached the end of In-Triple-World-Law cultivation. At the same time, this brings about a state very noticeable from its outer appearance: three flowers gathered above the head. A great deal of gong has been developed, all of which possesses a shape and form, and the energy column is now very high. The three flowers appear on the crown of the head, with one resembling a chrysanthemum and another a lotus. The three flowers spin individually and, at the same time, they revolve around each other. Each flower has a very tall pole atop it, reaching to the sky. These three poles also rotate and spin along with the flowers. A person feels that his head has grown heavy. By now, he has only taken the last step in the In-Triple-World-Law cultivation.

5. Mind-intent

Falun Gong cultivation carries no mind-intent. Mind-intent doesn't accomplish anything by itself, though it can send out commands. What is really at work are the supernormal abilities that have an intelligent being's ability to think and that can receive commands from the brain's signals. Yet many people, particularly those in the qigong community, have many different theories about it. They think mind-intent can accomplish many things. Some talk about using mind-intent to develop supernormal abilities, using it to open tianmu, to heal disease, perform teleportation, etc. This is an incorrect understanding. At lower levels, everyday people use mind-intent to direct the sensory organs and four limbs. At higher levels, a cultivator's mind-intent elevates a notch, directing abilities about. In other words, supernormal abilities are dictated by mind-intent. This is how we look at mind-intent. Sometimes we see a qigong master giving treatments to others. The patients say that they have become well without the master moving a finger, and they think the healing is through their mind-intent. In fact, that master uses a type of supernormal abilities and dictates it to give the treatment or to do whatever. Because supernormal abilities travel in a different dimension, everyday people cannot see them with their eyes. Those who don't know think it is the mind-intent that does the healing. Some people believe mind-intent can be used to heal disease, and this has misled people. This view must be clarified.

Human thoughts are a type of message, a type of energy, and a form of material existence. When people think, the brain produces a frequency. Sometimes it is very effective to chant a mantra. Why? Because the universe has its own vibrational frequency, and when the frequency of your mantra coincides with that of the universe, an effect will be produced. For it to be effective, it certainly must be a benign message since evil things are not allowed to exist in the universe. Mind-intent is also a specific type of thinking. The Law Bodies of a high-level qigong grand master are controlled and dictated by the thoughts of his main body. A Law Body also has his own thoughts and his own, independent ability to solve problems and carry out tasks. He is an entirely independent self. At the same time, a Law Body knows the thoughts of the qigong master's main body, and he carries out tasks according to those thoughts. For example, if the qigong master wants to treat a particular person, the Law Body will go there. Without that thought he will not go. When he sees an extremely good thing to do, he will do it on his own. Some masters haven't reached the state of enlightenment and there are things that they don't know yet, but which their Law Bodies already know.

"Mind-intent" also has another meaning, namely, inspiration. Inspiration doesn't come from one's main consciousness. The knowledge base of the main consciousness is very limited. When trying to come up with something that doesn't yet exist in this society, solely depending on the main consciousness won't work. Inspiration comes from the assistant consciousness. Some people are engaged in creative work or scientific research. When they get stuck after exhausting all of their brainpower, they put things aside, rest for a while, or take a walk outside. All of sudden, inspiration comes without their thinking. They immediately start to quickly write everything down, and thereby create something. This is because when the main consciousness is very strong, it controls the brain and, despite its effort, nothing comes forth. Once the main consciousness relaxes, the assistant consciousness starts to function and then controls the brain. Belonging to another dimension, the assistant consciousness is unrestrained by this dimension and is able to create new things. Yet the assistant consciousness cannot go beyond or interfere with the state of human society, and neither can it affect the process of society's development.

Inspiration comes from two sources. One is from the assistant consciousness. The assistant consciousness isn't blinded by this world and can produce inspiration. The other comes from the command and guidance of an intelligent being from higher levels. When guided by a higher-level intelligent being, people's minds are broadened and are able to create ground-breaking things. The entire development of society and the universe follow their own particular laws. Nothing happens by chance.

6. Levels of Cultivation in Falun Gong

(1) Cultivation at Higher Levels

Falun Gong cultivates at very high levels, so gong is generated quite rapidly. A great cultivation way is simple and easy to learn. From a broader perspective, Falun Gong has very few movements. Yet it controls all aspects of the body, including many things that are to be generated. As long as a person's xinxing keeps rising, his gong will grow very rapidly, as it doesn't require much intentional effort, the use of any particular method, setting up a bodily crucible and furnace to make dan from gathered medical drugs, or from adding fire and gathering medicinal drugs.[40] Relying on the guidance of mind-intent can be very complicated and make it easy for one to deviate. Here we provide the most convenient and best cultivation way, yet also the most difficult. In order for a cultivator to reach the state of the Milk-White Body through other methods, it would take more than a decade, several decades, or even longer. Yet we bring you to this stage immediately. This level might already pass by before you even feel it, as it might only last several hours. There will be one day when you will feel very sensitive, and only a little while later you won't feel as sensitive. In fact, you will have just passed a large level.

(2) Gong's Manifestations

After going through adjustment of the physical body, students of Falun Gong will reach the state that is suitable for cultivation of the Great Way *(Dafa)*: the state of the Milk-White Body. Gong will only develop after this state is reached. People with high-level tianmu can see that gong develops on the surface of a person's skin, and it is then absorbed into the practitioner's body. This process of gong generation and absorption keeps repeating itself, going layer by layer, sometimes very rapidly. This is gong of the first round. After the first round, the body of the practitioner is no longer a regular one. After reaching the Milk-White Body, one will never again get sick. Though similar to sickness, the pain that may emerge here and there, or the discomfort in a certain area is not sickness: It is caused by karma. After the second round

---

[40] A Taoist metaphor for internal alchemy.

of gong development, the intelligent beings will have grown very large and be able to move around and talk. Sometimes they are produced sparsely, sometimes in great density. They can also talk to each other. There is a great deal of energy stored in those intelligent beings, and this is used to change benti.

At a certain advanced level in Falun Gong cultivation, sometimes Cultivated Infants appear all throughout the body. They are very mischievous, enjoy playing, and are very kindhearted. Another kind of body can also be produced: the Immortal Infant. He sits on a lotus flower seat that is very beautiful. The Immortal Infant generated by cultivation is created by the merging of yin and yang within the human body. Both male and female cultivators are able to cultivate an Immortal Infant. Immortal Infant is very small in the beginning, and then gradually grows larger, ultimately growing to the cultivator's size. It looks exactly like him and is indeed there in his body. When people with supernormal abilities look at him, they will say that he has two bodies. Actually, he has succeeded in cultivating his benti. Additionally, many Law Bodies can be developed through cultivation. In short, all supernormal abilities that can be developed in the universe can be developed in Falun Gong; supernormal abilities developed in other cultivation methods are also all included in Falun Gong.

(3) Beyond-Triple-World-Law Cultivation

Through practice, practitioners make their meridians wider and wider, connecting them into one piece. That is, one cultivates to a state where there are no meridians or acupuncture points, or conversely, the meridians and acupuncture points will exist everywhere. This still doesn't mean that you have attained the Tao—it is only one type of manifestation in the process of Falun

Gong cultivation, the reflection of one level. When this stage is reached, the person will be at the end of In-Triple-World-Law cultivation. The gong developed will already be very powerful, and it will have fully taken shape. Additionally, the energy column will be very high, and the three flowers will appear atop the head. By now this person has merely taken the last step of In-Triple-World-Law cultivation.

Taking one step forward, there will be nothing left. All of one's gong will be pressed into the body's deepest dimension. One will enter the state of Pure White Body, wherein the body is transparent. With one more step forward, one will enter into Beyond-Triple-World-Law cultivation, also known as "cultivation of a Buddha's body." The gong developed at this stage belongs to the category of divine powers. At this point, one will have unlimited powers, becoming incredibly mighty. When reaching higher realms, one will cultivate to become a great enlightened being. This depends on how you cultivate your xinxing. Whichever level you cultivate to is the level of your Fruit Status. Dedicated cultivators acquire the righteous way, and obtain the Righteous Attainment, and this is the successful completion of cultivation.

Chapter III

Cultivation of Xinxing

All cultivators of Falun Gong must make cultivation of xinxing their top priority and regard xinxing as the key to developing gong. This is the principle of cultivation at higher levels. Strictly speaking, the energy potency that determines one's level isn't developed through practice, but through xinxing cultivation. Improving xinxing is easier said than done. Cultivators must be able to abandon many things, improve their enlightenment quality, bear sufferings upon sufferings, endure almost unendurable things, and so on. Why hasn't some people's gong grown, even though they have practiced for years? The fundamental causes are: first, they disregard xinxing; second, they do not know the righteous way of higher levels. This point must be brought to light. Many masters who teach gong talk about xinxing—they are teaching genuine things. Those who only teach movements and techniques without ever discussing xinxing actually teach evil cultivation. Practitioners must therefore exert great effort in improving their xinxing. Only then can they enter into high-level cultivation.

1. Xinxing's Inner Meaning

The "xinxing" referred to in Falun Gong cannot be fully summarized by "virtue *(de)*" alone. It encompasses much more than virtue *(de)*. It encompasses many different facets, including those of virtue *(de)*. Virtue *(de)* is only one manifestation of one's xinxing, so using only virtue *(de)* to understand the meaning of xinxing is inadequate. Xinxing encompasses how to deal with

53

the two issues of "gain" and "loss." "Gain" is to gain conformity to the characteristics of the universe. The characteristics that comprise the universe are Zhen, Shan, and Ren. A cultivator's degree of conformity to the characteristics of the universe is reflected in the individual's virtue *(de)*. "Loss" is to give up the negative thoughts and behaviors such as greed, personal gain, lust, desire, killing, fighting, theft, robbery, deception, jealousy, etc. If one is to cultivate toward higher levels, one also needs to abandon the pursuit of desires, something inherent in human beings. In other words, one should give up all attachments, and one should take lightly all personal gain and fame.

A complete person is composed of a physical body and a character. The same is true with the universe. In addition to the existence of substances, there also simultaneously exist the characteristics of Zhen, Shan, and Ren. Every particle of air contains these characteristics. In human society, these characteristics are reflected in the fact that good deeds are met with rewards and bad ones, punishment. At higher levels, the characteristics also manifest the states of supernormal abilities. People who align themselves with these characteristics are good people; those who depart from them are bad. People who comply with and assimilate to them are those who achieve the Tao. To conform to these characteristics, practitioners must have extremely high xinxing. Only this way can one cultivate toward higher levels.

It is easy to be a good person, but it is none too easy to cultivate xinxing—cultivators must prepare mentally. To rectify one's mind, sincerity is a prerequisite. People live in this world, where society has become very complicated. You want to do good deeds, but there are some people who don't want you to; you do not want to harm others, but others might harm you for various reasons. Some of these things happen for unnatural reasons. Will you understand

54

the reasons? What should you do? Being confronted with all the conflicts of this world, your xinxing is tested every moment. When confronted with indescribable humiliation, when your vital, self-interests have been infringed upon, when faced with money and lust, when in a power struggle, when rage and jealousy emerge in conflicts, when various conflicts in society and in the family take place, and when all kinds of suffering occur, can you always handle yourself in accordance with the strict xinxing requirement? Of course, if you can handle everything, you are already an enlightened being. Most practitioners start as everyday people after all, and cultivation of xinxing is gradual, moving upward little by little. Determined cultivators should be prepared to endure great suffering, and to face difficulties with a firm mind, and eventually they will attain the Right Fruit status. I hope that all of you cultivators maintain your xinxing well and improve your energy potency rapidly!

2. Loss and Gain

Both the communities of qigong and religion talk about loss and gain. Some people regard "loss" as being charitable, doing some good deeds, or giving a hand to people in trouble; they take "gain" to be gaining gong. Even monks in temples also say that one should be charitable. This understanding narrows the meaning of "loss." The "loss" we talk about, however, is much broader, and it is something of a larger scale. The things we require you to lose are the attachments of everyday people and the mind that doesn't let go of those attachments. If you can abandon the things you consider important and relinquish the things you think you cannot, that is "loss" in the truest sense. Offering help and displays of charity are only a part of "loss."

As an everyday person, one wants to have a little fame, personal gain, a better living standard, more comfort, and more money. These are everyday people's goals. As practitioners, we are different, for what we acquire is gong, not those things. We need to care less about personal gain and take it lightly, but we are not really asked to lose any material things; we cultivate in human society and need to live like everyday people. The key is for you to let go of your attachments—you are not really required to lose anything. Whatever belongs to you won't be lost, while the things that don't belong to you cannot be acquired. If acquired, they will have to be returned to others. To gain, you must lose. Of course, it's impossible to immediately handle everything very well, and neither is it possible to become an enlightened being overnight. Yet by cultivating little by little and improving step by step, it is attainable. You will gain however much you lose. On the issue of personal gains, you always take it lightly and would rather gain less in order to have peace of mind. You may suffer some losses when it comes to material things, but you will gain in terms of de and gong. This is where the truth lies. You are not to intentionally gain de and gong by exchanging fame, money, and personal gain. This should be understood further with your enlightenment quality.

A cultivator of the great Tao once said: "I don't want the things others want, and I don't possess the things others possess; however, I have things others don't, and I want things others don't." As an everyday person, a person hardly has a moment when he feels satisfied. He wants everything except for that rock that lies on the ground and that no one wants to pick up. Yet this Taoist cultivator said, "Then I'll pick up this rock." A proverb goes like this: "Rarity produces the precious, and scarcity bears the uniqueness." Rocks are worthless here, but most valuable in another dimension. This is a principle that an everyday person cannot understand. Many enlightened, high-level masters with great de have no material possessions. For them, there is nothing that cannot be relinquished.

The path of cultivation is the most correct, and practitioners are actually the most intelligent. The things that everyday people struggle for and the minute benefits they gain only last a short while. Even if you obtain through struggling, find something for free, or gain a little profit, so what? There is a saying among everyday people: When you are born, you cannot bring anything with you; when you die, you cannot take anything away with you. You enter the world with nothing, and you take nothing away when you leave it—even your bones will be burned to ashes. It doesn't matter if you have tons of money or are a dignitary—nothing can be taken with you when you leave. Yet gong can be taken since it grows on the body of your main consciousness. I am telling you that gong is hard earned. It is so precious and so hard to acquire that it cannot be exchanged for any amount of money. When your gong has reached a very advanced level, and if one day you should decide not to cultivate anymore, as long as you don't do anything bad, your gong will be converted into any material thing you want—you can have them all. But you will no longer have the things that cultivators possess, and will instead have only things that one can acquire in this world.

For the purpose of personal gain, some people acquire by improper means things that don't belong to them. Such a person thinks that he gets a good deal. The truth is that he gains such profit by exchanging his de with others, only he does not know it. For a practitioner, this has to be deducted from his gong; for a nonpractitioner, it has to be deducted from his life expectancy or something else. In short, the books will be balanced. This is the principle of the universe. There are also some people who always bully others, harm others with abusive words, and so on. When these actions take place, they throw a corresponding portion of their de to the other party, exchanging their de for the act of bullying others.

Some people think it is disadvantageous to be a good person. From the viewpoint of everyday people, they are at a disadvantage. What they acquire, however, is something that everyday people cannot: de, a white substance that is extremely precious. Without de, there will be no gong—this is an absolute truth. Why is it that many people cultivate but their gong fails to grow? It is precisely because they don't cultivate de. Many people talk about de and require practicing de, yet fail to disclose the real principles of how de is transformed into gong. It is left for individuals to comprehend. The close to ten thousand volumes of the Tripitaka and the principles that Sakyamuni taught for over forty some years all talked about one thing: de. The ancient books of Chinese Taoist cultivation all discussed de. The five thousand word book by Lao Zi, Tao Te Ching, also contemplated de. Yet some people still fail to understand it.

We talk about "loss." When you gain, you must lose. When you truly want to cultivate, you will encounter some tribulations. When they manifest in real life, one may experience a little suffering in the physical body or feel uncomfortable here and there—but it's not sickness. The tribulations can also manifest in society, in the family, or in the workplace—anything is possible. Conflicts will suddenly arise over personal gain or emotional friction, the goal of which is to enable you to improve xinxing. These things usually happen very suddenly and appear extremely intense. If you encounter something that is very tricky, embarrassing for you, that makes you lose face, or puts you in an awkward position, how are you going to handle it at that point? If you stay calm and unruffled—if you are able to do that—your xinxing will be improved through the tribulation and your gong will develop proportionately. If you can achieve a little, you will gain a little. However much you expend is however much you will gain. Typically, when we are in the middle of a tribulation, we might not be able to realize this, yet we must try. We shouldn't regard ourselves as everyday people; when conflicts arise, we should hold ourselves to higher standards. Since we cultivate among everyday people, our xinxing will be tempered among everyday people. We are bound to make some mistakes and to learn something from them. To not encounter any problems and just have your gong develop comfortably is impossible.

3. Simultaneous Cultivation of Zhen, Shan, and Ren

Our cultivation way cultivates Zhen, Shan, and Ren simultaneously. "Zhen" means to tell the truth, to do truthful things, to return to one's original, true self, and to ultimately become a true person. "Shan" means to develop great compassion, to do good things, and to save people. We particularly emphasize the ability of "Ren." Only with Ren can one cultivate to become a person with great de. Ren is a very powerful thing, transcending Zhen and Shan. During the entire process of cultivation, you are asked to forbear, to guard your xinxing, and not to act at will.

Being able to forbear when confronted with problems isn't easy. Some say, "If you don't hit back when beaten, don't talk back when slandered, or if you forbear even when you lose face in front of your family, relatives, and good friends, haven't you turned into Ah Q?![41] I say that if you act normal in all regards, your intelligence is no less than that of others, and you have only taken lightly the matter of personal gain, no one is going to say

---

[41] Ah Q (ah cue)—a foolish character in a Chinese novel.

you are stupid. Being able to forbear is not weakness, and neither is it being Ah Q. It is a display of strong will and self-restraint. There was a person in Chinese history, named Han Xin,[42] who once suffered the humiliation of crawling between someone's legs. That was great forbearance. There is an ancient saying: "When an everyday person is humiliated, he will draw his sword to fight." It means that when an ordinary person is humiliated, he will draw his sword to retaliate, swear at others, and throw punches at them. It's not an easy thing for one to come and live a lifetime. Some people live for their ego. It's not worth it whatsoever, and it is also too tiring. There is a saying in China: "With one step back, you'll discover a boundless sea and sky." Take a step back when you are confronted with problematic things. When you do, you will find a whole different scenario.

As a practitioner, you should not only show forbearance towards the people with whom you have conflicts and those who embarrass you in person, but also adopt a generous attitude and even thank them. If not for their conflicts with you, how could you improve your xinxing? How could the black substance be transformed into the white substance during suffering? How could you develop your gong? It is very hard when you are in the midst of a tribulation. Yet one must exercise self-restraint at that point, for as one's energy potency increases, the tribulations get continually stronger. It all depends on whether you can improve your xinxing. At the beginning, it may be upsetting to you, making you unbearably angry—so angry that your stomach or liver aches. Yet you don't erupt and are able to contain your anger—that is good. You have started to forbear, to intentionally forbear. You will then gradually and continuously improve your xinxing, truly taking these things lightly. It will be an even greater improvement

---

[42] Han Xin (hahn shin)—a leading general for Liu Bang in the Han Dynasty (206 B.C.-23 A.D.)

at that point. Everyday people take certain conflicts and minor problems very seriously. They live for ego and tolerate nothing. When angered to an unbearable point, they dare to do anything. Yet as a practitioner, you find very, very trivial—even too trivial—the things that people take seriously, because your goal is extremely long term and very far-reaching. You will live as long as this universe. When you again think about those things, it won't matter if you have them or not. When you think from a broader perspective, you can overcome all these things.

4. Eliminating Jealousy

Jealousy is a very big obstacle in cultivation, and it has a large impact on practitioners. It directly impacts a practitioner's energy potency, harms your fellow cultivators, and seriously interferes with our cultivation towards higher levels. As a practitioner, it must be eliminated one hundred percent. Although some people have cultivated to a certain level, they have yet to let go of their jealousy. Moreover, the harder it is to abandon, the easier it is for jealousy to grow stronger. The negative effects of this attachment make the improved part of one's xinxing vulnerable. Why is jealousy being singled out for discussion? Because jealousy is the strongest and most prominent thing which manifests among Chinese, weighing the most in people's minds. Nonetheless, many people are not aware of this. Called "Oriental jealousy" or "Asian jealousy," jealousy is characteristic of the East. The Chinese people are very introverted, very reserved, and don't express themselves openly, all of which easily leads to jealousy. Everything has two sides. Accordingly, an introverted personality has its pros and cons. Westerners are relatively extroverted. For instance, if a child scores a one hundred in school, he will happily call out on his way home, "I got a one hundred!" Neighbors will open their doors and windows to congratulate him, "Congratulations, Tom!" All of them will be happy for him. If this happens in China—think about it—people would feel disgusted once they heard it: "He scored a one hundred. So what? What's there to show off about?" The reaction is completely different when one has a jealous mentality.

Jealous types look down upon others and don't allow others to surpass them. When they see someone more capable than they, they begin to lose their balance, find it unbearable, and deny the facts. They want to get pay raises when others do, have an equal bonus, and share the same burden when something goes wrong. They get green-eyed and jealous when they see others making more money. Anyway, if others do better than they, they will find it unacceptable. Some people are afraid of accepting a bonus when they make certain achievements in their scientific research; they are afraid of others becoming jealous. People who have been awarded certain honors dare not reveal them, as they are afraid of jealousy and sarcasm. Some qigong masters cannot stand it when other qigong masters teach, so they go to make trouble for them. This is a xinxing problem. Suppose a group practices together. Some people have started later, yet have developed supernormal abilities. There are people who will then say: "What does he have to brag about? I've practiced for so many years and have a huge pile of certificates. How could he develop supernormal abilities before me?" There goes jealousy. Cultivation focuses inward. A cultivator should cultivate himself and find the causes of problems within himself. You should try to improve whatever area in which you haven't done enough, working hard on yourself. If you try to find the causes in others, you will be the only one left here after others complete cultivation and ascend. Won't you have wasted all of your time? Cultivation is for cultivating oneself!

Jealousy also harms fellow cultivators, such as when one's badmouthing makes it hard for others to enter tranquility; when such a person has supernormal abilities, he may, out of jealousy, use them to harm his fellow cultivators. For example, a person sits there, practicing, and he has been cultivating fairly well. Because he has gong, he sits there like a mountain. Then two beings float by, one of which used to be a monk who, because of jealousy, did not reach enlightenment; even though he possesses a certain energy potency, he has not reached completion. When they arrive at where the person is meditating, one says, "So-and-so is practicing here. Let's go around." But the other says, "In the past, I cut off a corner of Mount Tai." Then, he tries to hit the practitioner. Yet when he raises his hand, he cannot bring it down. Because the practitioner is cultivating the righteous way and has a protective shield, that being is unable to hit him. He wants to harm a cultivator of the righteous way, so it becomes a serious matter and he will be punished. People who are jealous harm themselves as well as others.

5. Abandoning Attachments

Having attachments refers to the relentless, zealous pursuit of a particular object or goal by practitioners who are unable to liberate themselves or too stubborn to heed any advice. Some people pursue supernormal abilities in this world, and this will certainly impact their cultivation toward higher levels. The stronger the sentiments, the more difficult they are to abandon, and the more unbalanced and unstable the feeling will become. Later on they will feel that they got nothing, and they will even start to doubt the things that they had been learning. Attachments stem from human desires. These attachments' attribute is that their target or goal is obviously limited, fairly clear, and specific, and frequently the person might be unaware of them himself. An everyday person has many attachments. In order to pursue something and obtain it, he might use any means necessary. A cultivator's attachments manifest differently, such as the pursuit of a particular supernormal ability, indulging in a certain vision, obsession with a certain manifestation, and so on. For a practitioner, no matter what you pursue it is incorrect—pursuit must be abandoned. The Tao School talks about nothingness. The Buddha School discusses emptiness and enters the gate of emptiness. Ultimately, we want to achieve the state of nothingness and emptiness, letting go of every attachment. Anything that you cannot let go of—such as the pursuit of supernormal abilities—must be abandoned. If you pursue them, that means you want to use them. In reality, that is the opposite of the characteristics of our universe. It is actually still an issue of xinxing. If you want to have it, then you actually want to flaunt it and show it off in front of others. That ability isn't something to showcase for others' viewing. Even if the purpose of your using them is very innocent and you just want to use them to do some good deeds, the good deeds that you would do could turn out to be none too good. It's not necessarily a good idea to handle matters of everyday people using supernormal means. After some people hear me remark that seventy percent of the class has had tianmu opened, they start to wonder, "Why can't I sense anything?" When they return home and practice, their attention focuses on tianmu, even to the point of getting a headache. In the end, they still cannot see anything. This is called an attachment. Individuals differ in physical state and inborn quality. They cannot possibly come to see through their tianmu at the same time, and neither can their tianmu be at the same level. Some people may be able to see and some may not. It is all normal.

Attachments are able to hinder and slow down the development of a cultivator's energy potency. In more serious cases, they may even result in practitioners taking an evil path. In particular, certain supernormal abilities may be used by people with inferior xinxing to do bad things. There have been cases where bad deeds were committed using supernormal abilities, due to a person's unreliable xinxing. Somewhere there was a male college student who developed the supernormal ability of mind control. With this he could use his own thoughts to manipulate the thoughts and conduct of others, and he used it to do bad things. When practicing, some people might witness visions appearing. They always want to have a clear look and total understanding. This is also a form of attachment. A certain hobby might become an addiction for some, and they are unable to shake it. That, too, is a form of attachment. Because of differences in inborn quality and purpose, some people cultivate in order to reach the highest level while some cultivate just to gain certain things. The latter mentality will surely limit the goal of cultivation. Without eliminating this kind of attachment, one's gong will not develop even if one practices. Therefore, practitioners should take all material gains lightly, pursue nothing, and let everything unfold naturally, thus avoiding the emergence of new attachments. This will depend upon the practitioner's xinxing. One cannot cultivate to enlightenment if one's xinxing is not fundamentally improved, or if any form of attachment is harbored.

6. Karma

(1) The Origin of Karma

Karma is a type of black substance that is the opposite of de. In Buddhism it is called "sinful karma," while here we call it "karma." Doing bad things is thus called "creating karma." Because of the wrong things that a person does in this life or past lives, karma is created. For instance, killing, bullying, fighting with others to obtain personal gain, gossiping about someone behind his back, being unfriendly to someone, and so on, can all create karma. In addition, some karma is passed on from ancestors, family relatives, or close friends. When one throws punches at someone else, he also throws his white substance over to the other person, and the vacated area in his body will be filled with the black substance. Killing is the worst evildoing—it is a wrongdoing and will add very heavy karma. Karma is the primary factor that causes sickness in people. Of course, it doesn't always manifest itself in the form of sickness—it can also manifest in the form of encountering some troublesome matters and so on. All of it is karma at work. Therefore, practitioners must not do anything bad. Any misconduct will produce bad messages, seriously impacting your cultivation.

Some people advocate collecting the qi of plants. When they teach their exercises, they also teach how to collect qi from plants; which tree has better qi and the colors of different trees' qi are discussed with intense interest. In a park in our northeastern region, some people practiced some kind of so-called qigong wherein they would roll all over the ground. After they would get up, they would circle around the pine trees and collect the qi of the pine trees. Within half a year the grove of pine trees had withered and turned yellow. This was a karma-generating act! It was also killing! Whether viewed from the perspective of our country's greening, the maintenance of ecological balance, or the perspective of a higher level, collecting qi from plants is not right. The universe is vast and boundless, with qi available everywhere for you to collect. Knock yourself out and go collect it—why abuse these plants? As a practitioner, where is your heart of mercy and compassion?

Everything has intelligence. Modern science already recognizes that plants have not only life, but also intelligence, thoughts, feelings, and even super-sensory capabilities. When your tianmu reaches the level of Law Eyesight, you will discover that the world is a totally different picture. When you go outside, rocks, walls, and even trees will talk to you. All objects have life. No sooner does an object form than does a life enter it. Organic and inorganic substances are categorized by people living on Earth. People living in temples get upset when they break a bowl, for the moment it is destroyed, its living being is released. It didn't finish its life journey, so it will have nowhere to go. It will therefore have extreme hatred towards the person who killed it. The angrier it gets, the more karma the person will accrue. Some "qigong masters" even go hunting. Where did their benevolence and compassion go? The Buddha and Tao Schools don't do things that violate heaven's principles of conduct. When one does these things, it is an act of killing.

Some people say that in the past they created a lot of karma, such as killing chickens or fish, fishing, etc. Does this mean that they can no longer cultivate? No, it does not. Back then, you did it without knowing the consequences, so it wouldn't have created more karma. Just don't do it anymore in the future, and that should be fine. If you do it again you are knowingly violating the principles, and that is not permitted. Some of our practitioners have this kind of karma. Your attendance in our seminar means that you have a predestined relationship, and you can cultivate upward. Shall we swat flies or mosquitoes when they come inside? As to your handling of this at your present level, it's not considered wrong if you swat them to death. If you cannot drive them out, then killing them is no big deal. When the time has come for something to die, naturally it will die. When Sakyamuni was still alive, he once wanted to take a bath and asked his disciple to clean the bathtub. The disciple discovered many bugs in the bathtub, so he returned and asked what he should do. Sakyamuni said it again, "It is the bathtub that I want you to clean." The disciple understood, and he went back and cleaned the bathtub. You shouldn't take certain things too seriously. We don't intend to make you an overly-cautious person. In a complicated environment it is not right, I think, if you are nervous every moment and afraid of doing something wrong. It would be a form of attachment—fear itself is an attachment.

We should have a compassionate and merciful heart. Handling things with a compassionate and merciful heart, we would be less likely to cause problems. Lighten up your self-interests, be kindhearted, and your compassionate heart will keep you away from wrongdoing. Believe it or not, you will discover that if you always hold a spiteful attitude and always want to fight and contend, you will even turn good things into bad ones. I often see some people who, when right, will not let others go; when he is right, he has finally found some grounds for punishing others. Similarly, we shouldn't stir up conflicts if we disagree with certain things. At times, the things you dislike may not necessarily be wrong. As a practitioner, when you upgrade your level continuously, every sentence you say will carry energy. You can control everyday people, so you cannot speak as you please. Particularly, when you are not able to see the truth of problems and their karmic relations, it is easy for you to commit wrongdoing and create karma.

(2) Eliminating Karma

The principles in this world are the same as those in heaven: You must eventually pay what you owe others. Even everyday people must also pay what they owe others. All the hardships and problems you encounter throughout your life result from karma. You have to pay. As to true cultivators, the paths of our lives will be altered. A new path that suits your cultivation will be arranged. Some of your karma will be reduced by your master, and what remains will be used to improve your xinxing. Through practice and the cultivation of xinxing, you exchange and pay for your karma. From now on, the problems you confront won't happen by chance, so please be mentally prepared. By enduring some tribulations, you will come to let go of all the things an everyday person cannot abandon. You will run into many troublesome matters. Problems will arise within the family, socially, and from other sources, or you may suddenly encounter disaster; it could even be that you get blamed for what is actually someone else's fault, and so on and so forth. Practitioners are not supposed to get sick, yet they may suddenly come down with serious sickness. It could come on with intense force, and they will suffer to the point where they can no longer bear it. Even hospital examinations yield no diagnosis. Yet later on, for an unknown reason, the sickness is gone without any treatment. In fact, the debt you owed is paid for in this manner. Perhaps one day, for no reason at all, your spouse starts a fight with you, losing his or her temper. Even very insignificant incidents may trigger big arguments. Afterwards, he or she will also feel confused over his or her loss of temper. As a practitioner, you should be clear as to why this kind of incident takes place: It is because that "thing" came, and it was asking you to pay for your karma. During such a moment, you must keep yourself under control and guard your xinxing to resolve it. Be appreciative and thankful that he or she has helped you pay for the karma.

After sitting in meditation for a long while, the legs will start to ache, sometimes with excruciating pain. People with tianmu at a higher level can see the following: when one is in great pain, there is a large chunk of the black substance—both inside and outside the body—coming down and being eliminated. The pain experienced when sitting in meditation is periodic and heart-piercing. Some understand it and are determined not to unfold their legs. The black substance will thus be eliminated and transformed into the white substance, and it, in turn, is transformed into gong. Practitioners cannot possibly pay for all their karma through sitting in meditation and practicing the exercises. They also need to improve their xinxing and enlightenment quality, and experience some tribulations. What is important is that we are compassionate. Compassion emerges very quickly in our Falun Gong. When sitting in meditation, many people find that tears start to fall for no reason. Whatever they think of, they feel grief. Whomever they look at, they see suffering. It is actually the heart of great compassion that has emerged. Your nature, your true self, starts to connect with the characteristics of the universe: Zhen, Shan, and Ren. When your compassionate nature emerges, you will do things with much kindness. From the inside out, you will be very kind. At that point, no one will bully you anymore. If someone did bully you at that point, your heart of great compassion would be effective and you wouldn't do the same to him in return. It is a type of power, the power that makes you different from everyday people.

When you encounter a tribulation, that great compassion will help you overcome it. At the same time, my Law Bodies will look after you and protect your life, but you must go through the tribulation. For example, when I was lecturing in Taiyuan there was an older couple that came to attend my class. They were in a hurry when crossing the street. When they were in the middle of the road, a car came speeding along, instantly knocking the elderly woman down, dragging her along more than ten meters. She finally fell down in the middle of the street. The car couldn't stop for another twenty meters. The driver got out of the car and said some rude words, and the passengers sitting inside the car also uttered some negative things. The old lady didn't say anything, and at that moment remembered what I had said. After she got up, she said, "Everything is all right, nothing is broken." She then went into the hall together with her husband. Had she said at that very moment, "Oh, it hurts here and it hurts there, too. You need to take me to the hospital," things would have turned out really bad. But she did not. The elderly woman said to me, "Master, I know what that was all about. It was helping me pay for my karma! A big chunk of karma and great tribulations have been paid for." You can imagine that she had very high xinxing and enlightenment quality. At such an advanced age and with the car going that fast, she was knocked down and dragged that far, finally falling heavily to the ground. Yet she got up, with a righteous mind.

Sometimes when a tribulation comes it seems tremendous— so overwhelming that there seems no way out. Perhaps it stays around for quite a few days. All of a sudden, a path appears, and things start to take a huge turn. In fact, it is because we have improved our xinxing and the problem has disappeared naturally.

In order to improve one's realm of mind, one must undergo all kinds of tests put forth by this world in the form of tribulations. If your xinxing has really improved and stabilized, during the process, karma will be eliminated; the tribulation will pass and your gong will develop. If during xinxing tests you fail to guard your xinxing and you conduct yourself improperly, do not be discouraged. Be proactive in gathering what you learn from this lesson, find where you fell short, and put effort into Zhen, Shan, and Ren. The next problem that will test your xinxing may come shortly thereafter. As your energy potency develops, the test of the next tribulation may come on even stronger and more suddenly. With every problem you overcome, your energy potency grows a little bit higher. If you are unable to overcome a problem, your gong will come to a standstill. Small tests lead to small improvements; big tests lead to big improvements. I hope that every practitioner is prepared to bear great suffering and has the determination and willpower to embrace hardships. You won't acquire real gong without expending effort. There is no principle in existence that will let you gain gong comfortably without any suffering or expending effort. If your xinxing doesn't change for the better and you still harbor personal attachments, you will never cultivate to become an enlightened being!

7. Demonic Interference

Demonic interference refers to the manifestations or visions that appear during the cultivation process and interfere with the practice. Their goal is to prevent practitioners from cultivating toward higher levels. In other words, demons come to collect debts.

When cultivation reaches a higher level, the issue of demonic interference will surely arise. It is inevitable that a person in his lifetime, and his ancestors in their lives, have committed some wrongdoing; this is called karma. Whether one's inborn quality is good or not determines how much karma this person carries with him. Even if he is a very good person, it is impossible for him to be free of karma. Because you don't practice cultivation, you cannot feel it. If your practice is only for healing and health improvement, the demons won't care. But once you begin cultivating to higher levels, they will bother you constantly. They can disturb you using many different methods, the goal of which is to prevent you from cultivating to higher levels and to make you fail in your cultivation practice. Demons present themselves in a variety of ways. Some do so in the form of daily life's happenings, while some interfere using messages from other dimensions. They dictate things to interfere with you every time you sit down, making it impossible to enter tranquility and, thus, also making it impossible to cultivate toward higher levels. Sometimes, the moment you sit down to meditate you start to feel sleepy or have all kinds of thoughts going through your mind, and you become unable to enter into a cultivation state. Other times, the moment you start practicing, your once-quiet surroundings suddenly fill with the noise of footsteps, doors slamming, cars honking, telephones ringing, and a variety of other forms of interference, making it impossible for you to become tranquil.

Another kind of demon is lust. During the practitioner's meditation or in his or her dreams, a beautiful woman or handsome man may appear in front of him or her. That person will entice you and seduce you, making stimulating gestures and attracting your attachment to sexual lust. If you cannot overcome it the first time, it will gradually escalate and continue to seduce you until you abandon the idea of cultivating to a higher level. This is a difficult test to pass, and quite a few practitioners have failed because of this. I hope you are mentally prepared for it. If someone didn't guard his xinxing well enough and failed once, he should truly learn a lesson from it. It will come and interfere again many times until you have truly maintained your xinxing and have completely let go of that attachment. This is a big hurdle that must be overcome. Otherwise, you will be unable to achieve the Tao and unable to successfully complete cultivation.

Another kind of demon presents itself during one's practice or in one's dreams. Some people suddenly see some horrifying faces that are ugly and real, or figures that are holding knives and threatening to kill. But they can only scare people. If they were to really stab, they wouldn't be able to touch the practitioner since Master has already installed a protective shield outside of the practitioner's body to keep him unharmed. They try to scare the person off so that he will stop cultivating. These only appear at one level or during one period of time, and they will pass very quickly—in a few days, a week, or a few weeks. It all depends on how high your xinxing is and how you treat this matter.

8. Inborn Quality and Enlightenment Quality

"Inborn quality" refers to the white substance one brings with him at birth. In fact, it is de- –a tangible substance. The more of this substance you bring with you, the better your inborn quality. People with good inborn quality more easily return to the truth and become enlightened, for they have no obstacles in their thinking. Once they hear about the study of qigong, or about things concerning cultivation, they immediately become interested and are willing to learn. They can connect with the universe. It is exactly as Lao Zi said: "When a wise man hears of the Tao, he will practice it diligently. When an average man hears of it, he will practice on and off. When a foolish man hears of it, he will laugh at it loudly. If he doesn't laugh loudly, it is not the Tao." Those people who can easily return to the truth and become enlightened are wise people. In contrast, for a person with a lot of black substance and an inferior inborn quality there is a barrier formed outside of his body, making it impossible for him to accept good things. If he comes into contact with good things, the black substance will make him disbelieve them. In fact, this is the role karma plays.

A discussion of inborn quality must involve the issue of enlightenment quality. When we talk about "enlightenment," some think that being enlightened is the equivalent of being smart. The "smartness" or "cunning" that everyday people refer to are indeed far different from the cultivation practice we are discussing. These types of "smart" people usually cannot attain enlightenment easily. They are only concerned with the practical, material world, so as to avoid being taken advantage of, and so as to avoid giving up any benefit. Most notably, a few individuals out there who regard themselves as knowledgeable, educated, and smart, think that cultivation practice is a fairy tale. To them, practicing exercises and cultivating xinxing are inconceivable. They consider practitioners foolish and superstitious. The enlightenment we speak of doesn't refer to being smart, but to the return of human nature to its true nature, being a good person, and conforming to the characteristics of the universe. Inborn quality determines one's enlightenment quality. If one's inborn quality is good, his enlightenment quality tends to be good, too. Inborn quality determines enlightenment quality; however, enlightenment quality isn't entirely dictated by inborn quality. No matter how good your inborn quality is, it is unacceptable if your understanding or comprehension is lacking. As to some individuals, their inborn quality isn't so good, yet they possess superb enlightenment quality and can thus cultivate to a higher level. Since we offer salvation to all sentient beings, we look at enlightenment quality, not inborn quality. Though you bring with you many bad things, as long as you are determined to cultivate to a higher level, this thought of yours is a righteous one. With this thought, you only need to give up a little bit more than others and you will eventually reach enlightenment.

A practitioner's body has already been purified. It will not contract illness after gong develops, because the presence of this high-energy substance in the body no longer permits the presence of the black substance. Some people just refuse to believe it, however, always thinking that they are sick, complaining, "Why am I so uncomfortable?" We say that what you have gained is gong. Having gained such a good thing, how can you not have discomfort? In cultivation, one has to give up things in exchange. In fact, those discomforts are all on the surface and have no impact whatsoever on your body. They appear to be sick, but they certainly are not. It all depends on how you understand it. Practitioners not only need to be able to bear the worst suffering, but also need to have good enlightenment quality. Some people don't even try to comprehend it when confronted with troubles. I am talking about higher levels and how people can measure themselves with higher criteria, yet they still treat themselves as everyday people. They cannot even make themselves enter the state of being true cultivators for the purpose of practicing, and neither can they believe that they will be at a higher level.

At a higher level, enlightenment refers to becoming enlightened; it is categorized into sudden enlightenment and gradual enlightenment. "Sudden enlightenment" refers to the process wherein the entire cultivation practice takes place in a locked mode. After you have completed the entire cultivation process and your xinxing has improved, at the last moment all supernormal abilities will be unleashed at once, tianmu will instantly open to the highest level, and your mind will be able to communicate with the higher-level beings in other dimensions. One will instantly be able to see the reality of the entire cosmos and its different dimensions and unitary paradises, and one will then be able to connect with them. One will also be able to use his great, supernatural powers. Sudden enlightenment is the most difficult path to take. In history, only people with superb inborn quality have been selected to become disciples, and it has been passed on privately and individually. It would be unbearable for average people! The path I took was sudden enlightenment.

The things I am imparting to you belong to gradual enlightenment. During the process of cultivation, when the time comes for a certain supernormal ability to develop, it will develop. But it is not assured that the emergent supernormal ability will be available for your use. When you have failed to improve your xinxing to a certain level and are unable to handle yourself properly, it is easy for you to commit wrongdoing. For the time being, these supernormal abilities will be unavailable for your use. Nonetheless, they will eventually be available to you. Through cultivation practice you will gradually improve your level and understand the truth of this universe. Just like with sudden enlightenment, completion will eventually be achieved. The path of gradual enlightenment is a little easier and takes no risks. The difficult part is that you see the entire cultivation process, so you should hold yourself to an even higher standard.

9. A Clear and Clean Mind

Some people cannot enter into tranquility during practice, and they search for a method. Some have asked me, "Master, why can't I be tranquil during practice? Can you teach me a method or technique so that I can become tranquil when I sit in meditation?" I say, how can you become tranquil?! Even if a deity were to come teach you a way, you would be unable to become tranquil. Why? The reason is that your own mind isn't clear and clean. Living in this society, with many emotions and desires, your various self-interests, and matters of your own or even of your family and friends have occupied too large a portion of your mind, commanding a high priority. How can you become tranquil when sitting in meditation? If you intentionally suppress something, it will come right back automatically.

Buddhism's cultivation speaks of precept, samadhi, and wisdom. Precept is to give up those things to which you are attached. Some adopt the approach of chanting the name of Buddha, which requires concentrated chanting to achieve the state of "one thought replacing thousands of others." Yet it's not simply an approach, but a type of ability. If you don't believe it, you should try chanting. I can promise you that when you use your mouth to chant the name of Buddha, other things will well up in your mind. It was Tibetan Tantrism that first taught about how to chant Buddha's name; chanting the name of the Buddha hundreds of thousands of times was required each day for a week. They would chant until they got dizzy, and then finally there was nothing left in their minds. This one thought had replaced all others. That is a type of ability that you might be incapable of performing. There are also some other methods of practice that teach you how to focus your thoughts on your dantian, or teach other methods, such as counting, fixating your eyes on objects, etc. As a matter of fact, none of these methods can make you enter into complete tranquility. Practitioners have to attain a clear and clean mind, give up their own self-interests, and let go of the heart of greed.

Actually, whether or not one can enter stillness and tranquility is a reflection of the height of one's ability and level. Being able to enter tranquility the moment you sit down is an indication of a high level. It is all right if for the time being you cannot become tranquil. You can slowly accomplish this during cultivation.

Xinxing improves gradually, as does gong. Without taking lightly your own self-interests and desires, there is no way for gong to develop.

Practitioners should hold themselves to higher standards at all times. Practitioners are continuously interfered with by all kinds of complicated social phenomena, many vulgar and unhealthy things, various emotions, and desires. The things that are promoted on television, in movies, and in literature induce you to become a stronger and more practical person among everyday people. If you cannot go beyond these, you will distance yourself even further from a cultivator's xinxing and mental state, acquiring less gong. Practitioners should have little or no dealings with those vulgar and unhealthy things. They should turn a blind eye and a deaf ear to these, being unmoved by people or things. I often say that the minds of everyday people cannot move me. I won't become happy when someone praises me, and neither will I get upset when someone yells at me. No matter how serious the xinxing interference among the everyday people may get, it has no effect on me. Practitioners should take very lightly all personal gain, not caring about it. At that point your intention to become enlightened will become solid. Without a strong attachment to the pursuit of fame and personal gain, and by regarding them as something inconsequential, you will not become frustrated or upset, and you will always stay psychologically balanced. Upon being able to abandon everything, you will naturally become clear and clean minded.

I have taught you the Great Way *(Dafa)* and all five sets of exercises. I have adjusted your bodies, installed Falun and energy mechanisms in your bodies, and my Law Bodies protect you. What should be given to you has all been given to you. During the class, it is all up to me. From this point on, it is all up to you.

"The master shows the entrance, while cultivation is up to the individual." As long as you study the Great Way thoroughly, attentively experience and comprehend it, guard your xinxing every moment, cultivate diligently, endure the worst sufferings of all, and forbear the worst of all hardships, I think you will surely succeed in your cultivation.

The path to cultivate gong lies in one's heart
The boat to sail the boundless Dafa rides on suffering

Chapter IV
Falun Gong Practice System

Falun Gong is a special cultivation practice of the Buddha School. It has unique parts that distinguish it from other regular cultivation methods of the Buddha School. Falun Gong is an advanced cultivation practice system. In the past it served as a rigorous cultivation method that demanded that its practitioners have extremely high xinxing or great inborn quality. For this reason the cultivation practice system is difficult to popularize. Nonetheless, in order for more practitioners to improve their levels, for them to know about this cultivation system, and to meet the needs of these numerous, devoted practitioners, I have compiled a set of cultivation exercises suitable for the public. In spite of the modifications, these exercises still far exceed average cultivation systems in terms of their offerings and the levels at which they are practiced.

Falun Gong practitioners can not only develop quickly their energy potency and supernormal abilities, but also acquire an incomparably powerful Falun in a very short period of time. Once formed, the Falun perpetually rotates automatically in a practitioner's lower abdomen. It continuously collects energy from the universe and transforms it into gong in practitioner's benti. The goal of "the Fa refines the practitioner" is thus achieved.

Falun Gong consists of five sets of movements. They are the following exercises: Buddha Showing A Thousand Hands, Falun Standing Stance, Penetrating the Two Cosmic Extremes, Falun Heavenly Circuit, and Way of Strengthening Divine Powers.

1. Buddha Showing A Thousand Hands Exercise *(Fo Zhan Qian Shou Fa)*[43]

Principle:

The core of Buddha Showing A Thousand Hands Exercise is stretching to open up all energy channels. Beginners can acquire energy in a short period of time after practicing this exercise, and experienced practitioners will improve quickly. This exercise requires all energy channels to be opened up at the outset, enabling practitioners to immediately practice at a very high level. The movements of this exercise are quite simple because the Great Tao is, as a rule, simple and easy to learn. Though the movements are simple, on a larger scale they control many things evolved by the entire cultivation system. When practicing this exercise, one's body will feel warm and will experience a unique sensation of there being a very strong energy field. This is caused by stretching and opening all the energy channels throughout the body. The purpose is to break through areas where the energy is blocked, to enable energy to circulate freely and smoothly, to mobilize the energy within the body and under the skin, circulating it vigorously, and to absorb a great amount of energy from the universe. It simultaneously enables the practitioner to quickly enter the state of having a qigong energy field. This exercise is practiced as the basic exercise of Falun Gong, and it is usually done first. It is one of the methods for strengthening cultivation.

Verse *(Kou Jue)*[44]

---

[43] Fo Zhan Qian Shou Fa (foah jhan chyen show fah)

[44] Kou Jue (ko jueh) – "mnemonic rhyme"; here, a verse recited before performing the exercise.

身 神 合 一　　動 靜 隨 機
Shen Shen He Yi　　Dong Jing Sui Ji
(shun shun huh ee)　　(dong jing sway jee)

頂 天 獨 尊　　千 手 佛 立
Ding Tian Du Zun　　Qian Shou Fo Li
(ding tyen doo zun)　　(chyen show fwuo lee)

Preparation:

Relax the entire body, but do not become too loose. Stand naturally, with feet shoulder-width apart. Bend the knees slightly. Keep the knees and hips relaxed. Tuck your chin in slightly. The tip of the tongue touches the upper palate.[45] Leave a little space between the teeth. Close the lips and gently shut the eyes. Maintain a serene expression on the face. During the practice you will have the feeling that you are very big and tall.

Conjoin the Hands (Liang Shou Jieyin)[46]

Raise both hands with the palms facing upwards. The thumb tips slightly touch each other. Join the other four fingers and overlap them on top of each other. For males the left hand is on top; for females the right hand is on top. The hands form an oval shape and are held at the lower abdomen area. Keep both upper arms slightly forward with the elbows suspended so the underarms are open (see Fig. 1-1).

Maitreya Stretching His Back (Mi Le Shen Yao)[47]

Begin with hands conjoined (jieyin). While raising the conjoined

---

[45] upper palate: the ridge behind the upper teeth.

[46] Liang Shou Jie Yin (lyang show jyeh yin)

[47] Mi Le Shen Yao (me luh shun yow)

Fig. 1-1   Fig. 1-2

hands, straighten both legs gradually. When the hands reach the front of the face, separate them and turn both palms upward gradually. Once the hands are above the top of the head, the palms face upward and the fingers of both hands point toward each other at a distance of 20-25 cm (8-10 inches) (see Fig. 1-2). At the same time, push the head upward and press the feet downward on the ground. Press up hard with the base of both palms and stretch the body for about 2 to 3 seconds. Then, immediately relax the whole body; in particular, the knees and hips should return to the relaxed state.

Fig. 1-3   Fig. 1-4

Tathagata Pouring Energy into the Top of the Head (*Ru Lai Guan Ding*)[48]

Follow the above posture. Turn both palms outward 140° to both sides simultaneously, so that the inside of the wrists face each other, forming the shape of a "funnel." Straighten the wrists and move them downward (see Fig. 1-3).

When the hands reach the front of the chest, the palms face the chest at a distance of about 10 cm (4 inches). Continue moving both hands down to the lower abdomen (see Fig. 1-4).

---

[48] Ru Lai Guan Ding (roo lie gwan ding)

Fig. 1-5

Press the Hands Together in Front of the Chest (*Shuang Shou Heshi*)[49]

When reaching the lower abdominal area, immediately lift the hands up to the chest and press them together *(heshi)* (Figure 1-5). When putting the hands together, the fingers and the base of the palms are pressed against each other with a hollow space between the palms. Hold the elbows up, with the forearms forming a straight line. (Keep hands in the Lotus Posture,[50] except when putting hands together *(heshi)* or conjoining them *(jieyin);* this is the same for the following exercises.)

---

[49] Shuan Shou He Shi (shwang show huh shr)
[50] Lotus Posture – a hand posture in which the middle finger protrudes slightly inwards, remaining mostly straight.

86

Fig. 1-6   Fig. 1-7

Hands Pointing to Heaven and Earth *(Zhang Zhi Qian Kun)*[51]

Begin with the posture of heshi. Simultaneously separate the two hands 2-3 cm (1 inch) apart, and start to turn them. Males turn the left hand (female the right hand) towards the chest and turn the right hand outwards, so that the left hand is on top and the right hand is at the bottom. Both hands are in a straight line with the forearms (see Fig. 1-6).

Next, stretch the left forearm diagonally to the upper left with the palm facing down, until the hand reaches the level of the head. The right hand is still at the chest with the palm facing up. As the left hand is extended, stretch the entire body gradually, push the head upward, and press the feet downward. Stretch the left hand

---

[51] Zhang Zhi Qian Kun (jhang jhur chyen kuhn)

87

Fig. 1-8   Fig. 1-9

upward in the upper left direction, while the right hand that is in front of the chest stretches outward together with the upper arm (see Fig. 1-7). Stretch for about 2 to 3 seconds, and then immediately relax the entire body. Move the left hand to the front of the chest and to heshi (see Fig. 1-5).

Next, turn the palms again. The right hand (female the left hand) is on top and the left hand is at the bottom (see Fig. 1-8).

The right hand repeats the previous movements of the left hand; that is, extend the right forearm diagonally upward with the palm facing down, until the hand has reached as high as the head. The left hand is still at chest with the palm facing upward. After stretching (see Fig. 1-9), immediately relax the entire body. Move the hands in front of the chest and put them together in

88

Fig. 1-10

heshi (see Fig. 1-5).

Golden Monkey Splitting Its Body (*Jin Hou Fen Shen*)[52]

Begin with the posture of heshi. Separate the hands at the chest and extend them toward the sides of the body, forming a straight line with the shoulders. Gradually stretch the entire body. Push the head upward, press the feet downward, straighten the two hands forcefully at the sides, and stretch in four directions (see Fig. 1-10) for 2-3 seconds. Immediately relax the entire body and put the hands together in heshi (see Fig. 1-5).

---

[52] Jin Hou Fen Shen (jin ho fun shun)

Fig. 1-11

Two Dragons Diving into the Sea *(Shuang Long Xia Hai)*[53]

From the posture of heshi, separate hands and extend them down towards the lower front. When the two arms are parallel and straight, they should form an angle of about 30° with the legs (see Fig. 1-11). Stretch the entire body. Push the head upward and press the feet downward. Stretch for about 2-3 seconds. Relax the entire body instantly. Draw back the two hands and put them together in heshi.

Bodhisattva Placing Hands on Lotus *(Pu Sa Fu Lian)*[54]

From the posture of heshi, separate both hands and extend them

---

[53] Shuang Long Xia Hai (shwang long shia high)
[54] Pu Sa Fu Lian (poo sah foo lyen)

Fig. 1-12

diagonally to the sides of the body, with the angle between the arms and the legs at about 30° (see Fig. 1-12). Stretch the whole body gradually, while the fingertips stretch out downward with a little force. Then, relax the entire body immediately. Move the hands to the chest and put them together in heshi.

Arhat Carrying a Mountain on His Back *(Luo Han Bei Shan)*[55]

Begin with the hands in heshi. Separate the hands and extend them to the back of the body. Meanwhile, turn both palms to face backward. When the hands are passing the sides of the body, flex the wrists slowly. When the hands reach behind the body, the

---

[55] Luo Han Bei Shan (loah hahn bay shon)

Fig. 1-13

angle between the wrists and the body is 45° (see Fig. 1-13).
Stretch the entire body gradually. After the two hands reach the
proper position, push the head upward and press the feet
downward. Keep the body upright, and stretch for about 2-3
seconds. Relax the entire body immediately. Draw back the hands
and return the hands to heshi.

Vajra Toppling a Mountain (*Jin Gang Pai Shan*)[56]

Begin with the hands together in heshi. Separate both hands and
push them forward with the palms. The fingers point up. Keep
the arms at shoulder level. After the arms are straightened, push
the head upward and press the feet downward. Keep the body

---

[56] Jin Gang Pai Shan (jin gahng pie shon)

Fig. 1-14

upright (see Fig. 1-14). Stretch for 2-3 seconds. Immediately relax the entire body. Put the two hands together in front of the chest and return the hands together to heshi.

Overlap the Hands in front of the Lower Abdomen *(Die Kou Xiao Fu)*[57]

Begin with the hands together in heshi. Slowly move the hands downward, turning the palms to face the abdominal area. When the hands reach the lower abdominal area, overlap the hands. For males, the left hand is inside, for female, the right hand is inside. The palm of one hand faces the back of the other. Keep a distance

---

[57] Die Kou Xiao Fu (diah ko shyow foo)

93

Fig. 1-15   Fig. 1-16

of 3 cm (1 inch) between the two hands and another 3 cm (1 inch) between the inner hand and the lower abdomen. One usually overlaps the hands for 40 to 100 seconds (see Fig. 1-15). Finish the exercise by conjoining the two hands in jieyin posture (see Fig. 1-16).

2. The Falun Standing Stance Exercise *(Falun Zhuang Fa)*[58]

Principle:
This is the second set of Falun Gong exercises. It is a tranquil standing exercise composed of four wheel-embracing movements. The movements are repetitive, and each posture needs to be held for quite a long time. Beginners' arms may initially feel heavy and sore. After the practice, however, their entire body will feel relaxed, without feeling any of the fatigue that comes from working. As the frequency and length of practice increase, practitioners can feel a Falun rotating between the two arms. Frequent practice of the Falun Standing Stance will enable the entire body to completely open, and it will enhance the energy potency. Falun Standing Stance is a comprehensive cultivation method to increase wisdom, upgrade levels, and strengthen divine powers. The movements are simple, yet much can be achieved from this exercise; what it practices is all-inclusive. During practice, do the movements naturally. You must be aware that you are practicing. Do not sway, though it is normal to move slightly. As with the other exercises of Falun Gong, the end of this exercise does not mean the end of the practice since Falun never stops rotating. The duration of each movement may differ from person to person; the longer, the better.

Verse

生 慧 增 力　　融 心 輕 體
Sheng Hui Zeng Li　Rong Xin Qing Ti
(shung hway zung lee) (rong shin ching tee)

似 妙 似 悟　　法 輪 初 起
Si Miao Si Wu　　Fa Lun Chu Qi
(szz myao szz woo)　(fah luhn chew chee)

---

[58] Falun Zhuang Fa (fah-luhn jwang fah)

95

Fig. 2 1

Preparation:

Relax the entire body, but do not become too loose. Stand naturally, with feet shoulder-width apart. Bend the knees slightly. Keep the knees and hips relaxed. Tuck your chin in slightly. The tip of the tongue touches the upper palate. Leave a little space between the teeth. Close the lips and gently shut the eyes. Maintain a serene expression on the face. Conjoin the hands in jieyin (see Fig. 2-1).

Holding the Wheel in front of the Head *(Tou Qian Bao Lun)*[59]

Start with the hands in jieyin. Slowly raise both hands from the lower abdomen while separating them. When the hands have reached the front of the head, the palms are facing the face at the

---

[59] Tou Qian Bao Lun (toe chyen baow luhn)

Fig. 2-2   Fig. 2-3

eyebrow level. The fingertips of both hands point to each other, 15 cm (5 inches) apart. The two arms form a circle and the entire body is relaxed (see Fig. 2-2).

Holding the Wheel in front of the Abdomen (*Fu Qian Bao Lun*)[60]

Move both hands gradually downward from the previous position. Keep the posture unchanged until they reach the lower abdominal area. Keep a distance of about 10 cm (4 inches) between the hands and the abdomen. Hold the two elbows forward, keeping the underarms open. The palms face up. The fingers of both hands point to each other, 10 cm (4 inches) apart. The arms form a circle (as Fig. 2-3).

---

[60] Fu Qian Bao Lun (foo chyen baow luhn)

Fig. 2-4   Fig. 2-5

Holding the Wheel above the Head *(Tou Ding Bao Lun)*[61]

From the previous position, raise the hands slowly, keeping the circular shape of the arms unchanged. Hold the wheel above the head with the fingers pointing toward each other. The palms face downward, keeping a distance of 20-30 cm (8-12 inches) between the fingertips of the two hands. The arms form a circle. Keep the shoulders, arms, elbows and wrists relaxed (see Fig. 2-4).

Holding the Wheel on Both Sides of the Head *(Liang Ce Bao Lun)*[62]
Slowly move the hands downward from the previous position to

---

[61] Tou Ding Bao Lun (toe ding baow luhn)

[62] Liang Ce Bao Lun (lyang tseh baow luhn)

98

Fig. 2-6   Fig. 2-7

the sides of the head. Keep the palms facing both ears, the forearms upright, and the shoulders relaxed. Do not keep the hands too close to the ears (see Fig. 2-5).

Overlap the Hands in Front of the Lower Abdomen *(Die Kou Xiao Fu)*

Slowly move both hands down from the previous position to the lower abdomen. Overlap the hands (see Fig. 2-6).
Finish the exercise with hands in jieyin posture (see Fig. 2-7).

3. Penetrating the Two Cosmic Extremes Exercise *(Guantong Liang Ji Fa)*[63]

Principle:

This exercise is intended to mix and merge the cosmic energy with the energy inside of one's body. A great amount of energy is expelled and taken in. In a very short time, the practitioner can expel the pathogenic and black Qi from his body and take in a great deal of energy from the cosmos, enabling his body to be purified and to quickly reach the state of "a Pure-White Body." While doing the hand movements, this exercise also facilitates the "opening of the top of the head," and it unblocks the passages under the feet.

Before doing the exercise, imagine yourself as two large empty barrels standing up between heaven and earth, gigantic and incomparably tall. With the upward movement of the hands, the qi inside the body rushes directly out of the top of the head to the upper extreme of the cosmos; with the downward movement of the hands, it goes out through the bottom of the feet to the lower extreme of the cosmos. Following the movements of the hands, the energy returns to the inside of the body from both extremes, and it is then emitted in the opposite direction. Repeat the movements alternately nine times. At the ninth movement, hold the left hand (right hand for females) up and wait for the arrival of the other hand. Next, both hands move downward together, bringing the energy to the lower extremes, and then back to the upper extremes along the body. After the hands move up and down nine times, the energy is brought back into the body. Turn Falun clockwise (viewed from the front) at the lower abdomen four times to spin the energy that is outside back into the body. Conjoin the hands in jieyin to end the exercise, but not the practice.

---

[63] Guangtong Liang Ji Fa (gwang-tong lyang jee fah)

Fig. 3-1   Fig. 3-2

Verse

淨 化 本 體
Jing Hua Ben Ti
(jing hwa bun tee)

法 開 頂 底
Fa Kai Ding Di;
(fah kigh ding dee)

心 慈 意 猛
Xin Ci Yi Meng
(shin tsz ee mung)

通 天 澈 地
Tong Tian Che Di
(tong tyen chuh dee)

Preparation:

Relax the entire body, but do not become too loose. Stand naturally, with feet shoulder-width apart. Bend the knees slightly. Keep the knees and hips relaxed. Tuck your chin in slightly. The tip of the

101

Fig. 3-3   Fig. 3-4

tongue touches the upper palate. Leave a little space between the teeth. Close the lips and gently shut the eyes. Assume a serene expression on the face. Conjoin the hands in jieyin (Fig. 3-1), then put them together in heshi in front of the chest (see Fig. 3-2).

Single-Hand Movement *(Dan Shou Chong Guan)[64]*

From having the heshi posture, start with a single-hand movement. The hands move slowly along with the energy mechanism outside of the body. Following the movements of hands, the energy inside the body flows up and down continuously. For males, lift the left hand upward first; for females, lift the right hand upward first (see Fig. 3-3).

---

[64] Dan Shou Chong Guan (dahn show chong gwan)

Fig. 3-5   Fig. 3-6

Slowly lift the hand, passing along the front side of the face and extend it beyond the top of the head. Simultaneously, slowly lower the right hand (the left hand for female). Keep the two hands moving alternately in this way (see Fig. 3-4). Keep both palms facing the body at a distance of 10 cm *(4 inches)*. In doing the exercise, keep the entire body relaxed. One up-and-down movement of the hand is counted as one time. Repeat for a total of nine times.

Double-Hand movement (Shuang Shou Chong Guan)[65]

At the ninth single-hand movement, the left hand (right hand for females) stays up and waits while one lifts the other hand. Both

---

[65] Shuang Shou Chong Guan (shwang show chong gwan)

Fig. 3-7   Fig. 3-8

hands are pointing upward (see Fig. 3-5).

Next, move both hands downward at the same time (see Fig. 3-6). Keep the palms facing the body at a distance of 10 cm *(4 inches)*. One up-and-down movement of the hands is counted as one time. Repeat for nine times.

Turning Falun with Two Hands *(Shuang Shou Tui Dong Falun)*[66]

After completing the double-hand movements, move both hands downward past the face and over the chest until reaching the location of the lower abdomen. Now turn Falun at the lower

---

[66] Shuang Shou Tui Dong Falun (shwang show tway dong fah-luhn)

Fig. 3-9   Fig. 3-10

abdomen (see Fig. 3-7, 3-8, and 3-9), with the left hand inside for males and the right hand inside for females. Keep a distance of 3 cm *(1 inch)* between both the two hands and between the inner hand and the lower abdomen. Turn Falun clockwise (viewed from the front) four times to spin the energy from outside back to the inside of the body. While turning the Falun, keep the movements of the two hands within the area of the lower abdomen.

Conjoin the Hands (see Fig. 3-10) *(Liang Shou Jieyin)*

105

4. Falun Heavenly Circuit Exercise *(Falun Zhou Tian Fa)*[67]

Principle:

This exercise enables the human body's energy to circulate over large areas. Rather than going through only one or several meridians, the energy circulates from the entire yin side of the body to the yang side, over and over again. This exercise is much superior to the average methods of opening up the meridians or the great and small heavenly circuits. It is an intermediate-level exercise of Falun Gong. On the basis of the previous three sets of exercises, this one is intended to open up all meridians throughout the body (including the great heavenly circuit) so that the meridians will gradually be connected throughout the entire body, from top to bottom. The most outstanding feature of this exercise is its use of Falun's rotation to rectify all abnormal conditions of the human body, enabling the human body—the small cosmos—to return to its original state, and the whole body's energy can circulate freely and smoothly. Upon reaching this state, the practitioner will have achieved a very high level of cultivation of In-Triple-World-Law. Those with great inborn quality can begin their cultivation of the Great Way *(Dafa)*. At this time their energy potency and divine powers will grow dramatically. When practicing this exercise, move the hands along with the energy mechanism. Each movement is unhurried, slow, and smooth.

Verse

旋 法 至 虛　　心 輕 似 玉
Xuan Fa Zhi Xu　　Xin Qing Si Yu
(shwen fah jhr shyew) (shin ching szz yew)

---

[67] Falun Zhou Tian Fa (fah-luhn joe tyen fah)

Fig. 4-1   Fig. 4-2

返 本 歸 真　悠 悠 似 起
Fan Ben Gui Zhen   You You Si Qi
(fahn bun gway jhun) (yo yo szz chi)

Preparation:

Relax the entire body, but do not become too loose. Stand naturally, with feet shoulder-width apart. Bend the knees slightly. Keep the knees and hips relaxed. Tuck your chin in slightly. The tip of the tongue touches the upper palate. Leave a little space between the teeth. Close the lips and gently shut the eyes. Maintain a serene expression on the face.

Conjoin the hands in jieyin (see Fig. 4-1), then put the hands together heshi in front of the chest (see Fig. 4-2).

107

Fig. 4-3   Fig. 4-4

Separate the two hands from heshi. Move them down toward the lower abdomen while turning both palms to face the body. Keep a distance of about 10 cm *(4 inches)* between the hands and the body. After the hands have passed along the lower abdomen, stretch them further downward along the inner sides of the two legs. At the same time, bend at the waist and squat down (see Fig. 4-3).

When the fingertips are close to the ground, slide the hands along the outside of both feet to draw a circle from the front of each foot to the outside of the heel (see Fig. 4-4).

Fig. 4-5   Fig. 4-6

Then, bend both wrists slightly and lift the hands up along the back of the legs (see Fig. 4-5).

Straighten the spine while lifting the hands up along the back (see Fig. 4-6). During the exercise, do not let the two hands touch any part of the body; otherwise, the energy on both hands will be taken back into the body.

109

Fig. 4-7 Fig. 4-8

When the hands can not be lifted any higher, make hollow fists (see Fig. 4-7), then pull the hands forward passing through the underarms.

Cross the two arms in front of the chest; (There is no special requirement for which arm is above or which arm is below. It depends on one's habit. This is the same for both males and females) (see Fig. 4-8).

Fig. 4-9   Fig. 4-10

Open the hollow fists and place the two hands over the shoulders (leaving a gap). Move both hands along the outside *(yang side)* of the arms. When reaching the wrists, turn the hands so the palms face each other at a distance of 3-4 cm (1 inch). That is, the outer thumb is now turned to be on top and the inner thumb is below. At this time, the hands and the arms form a "straight line" (see Fig. 4-9).

Turn both palms as if holding a ball; that is, the outside hand turns inside and the inside hand turns outside. As both hands push along the insides *(yin side)* of the lower and upper arms, raise them up and over the back of the head. The hands remain in a crossed position at the back of the head (see Fig. 4-10).

Fig. 4-11   Fig. 4-12

Next, continue to move the hands further down toward the backbone (see Fig. 4-11).

Separate the two hands with the fingertips pointing downward, and connect with the energy of the back. Then move both hands in parallel over the top of the head to the front of the chest (see Fig. 4-12). A heavenly circuit is thus completed. Repeat the movements nine times. After completing the exercise, move the two hands down along the chest to the lower abdomen.

Fig. 4-13   Fig. 4-14

Overlap the two hands in front of the lower abdomen *(die kou xiao fu)* (see Fig. 4-13), and then conjoin the two hands in jieyin (see Fig. 4-14).

5. Strengthening Divine Powers Exercise *(Shen Tong Jia Chi Fa)*[68]

Principle:

The Strengthening Divine Powers Exercise is a tranquil cultivation exercise in Falun Gong. It is a multi-purpose practice intended to strengthen one's divine powers (including supernormal abilities) and energy potency by turning Falun with the Buddha's hand gestures. This exercise is above the intermediate-level and was originally kept as a secretive practice. In order to meet the demands of practitioners with a substantial foundation, I have specially made public this cultivation method to save those predestined practitioners. This exercise requires sitting with both legs crossed. The full-lotus position is preferred, though the half-lotus position is also acceptable. During the practice, the flow of qi is strong and the energy field around the body is quite large. The hands move to follow the energy mechanism installed by Master. When the hand movements start, the heart follows the movement of the thoughts. When strengthening the divine powers, keep the mind empty, with a slight focus on both palms. The center of the palms will feel warm, heavy, electric, numb, as if holding a weight, etc. Nevertheless, do not pursue any of these sensations intentionally—just let it happen naturally. The longer the legs are crossed, the better; it depends on one's endurance. The longer one sits, the more intense the exercise is and the faster the energy grows. When doing this exercise, do not think of anything—there is no mind-intent—and ease into tranquility. Gradually enter into the state of Ding *(tranquil yet conscious state of mind)* from the dynamic state that seems tranquil but is not Ding. Your main consciousness, however, must be aware that you are practicing.

---

[68] Shen Tong Jia Chi Fa (shun tong jya chr fah)

114

Fig. 5-1

Verse

有 意 無 意　　　印 隨 機 起
You Yi Wu Yi　　　Yin Sui Ji Qi
(yo　ee　woo　ee)　　(yin sway jee chi)

似 空 非 空　　　動 靜 如 意
Si Kong Fei Kong　Dong Jing Ru Yi
(szz kong fay kong)　(dong jing roo ee)

Conjoin the Hands (*Liang Shou Jieyin*)

Sit with legs crossed in lotus position. Relax the entire body, but do not become too loose. Keep the waist and neck upright. Draw the lower jaw in slightly. The tip of tongue touches the upper

115

Fig. 5-2   Fig. 5-3

palate. Leave a space between teeth. Close the lips. Gently shut the eyes. Fill the heart with compassion. Assume a peaceful and serene expression on the face. Conjoin the hands in jieyin at the lower abdomen, and gradually ease into tranquility (see Fig. 5-1).

First Hand Gesture

When the hand movements start, the heart follows the movement of the thoughts. Movements should follow the energy mechanism installed by Master. They should be carried out unhurriedly, slowly, and smooth. Slowly raise both hands in the jieyin position until reaching the front of the head. Then, gradually turn the palms to face upward. When the palms are face-up, the hands have also reached the highest point (see Fig. 5-2).

116

Fig. 5-4   Fig. 5-5

Next, separating the two hands, draw an arc over the head, rotating toward the sides until reaching the front side of the head (see Fig. 5-3).

Immediately after, slowly drop both hands. Try to hold the elbows inward, with palms facing upward and fingers pointing toward the front (see Fig. 5-4).

Next, flex both wrists and cross them in front of the chest. For males, the left hand travels outside, for females, the right hand travels outside (see Fig. 5-5).

When a "straight line" is formed by the arms and hands, the wrist of the hand on the outside rotates outwardly, with the palm turned to face upward. Draw a semicircle, and turn the palm to

Fig. 5-6   Fig. 5-7

face upward with fingers pointing toward the back. The hand uses a little force. The palm of the hand that is inside after crossing over in front of the chest turns to face downward. Straighten the arm. Rotate the arm and hand so the palm faces outward. The hands and arms in the lower front of the body should form an angle of 30° with the body (see Fig. 5-6).

Second Hand Gesture

Following the previous position (see Fig. 5-6), the left hand (the upper hand) moves to the inside. The palm of the right hand turns toward the body as the right hand moves up. The movement is the same as in the first gesture, with the left and right hands switched. Hand positions are exactly opposite (see Fig. 5-7).

Fig. 5-8   Fig. 5-9

Third Hand Gesture

Straighten the right wrist for males (left for females) with the palm facing the body. After the right hand moves across in front of the chest, turn the palm to face down and move down till the lower front where the shin is located. Keep the arm straight. The left wrist for males (right for females) turns while moving up and crossing the right hand so the palm faces the body. At the same time, move the palm toward the left (right for females) shoulder. When the hand has reached its position, the palm faces up and the fingers point to the front (see Fig. 5-8).

Fourth Hand Gesture

It is the same gesture as shown above with hand positions

119

Fig. 5-10   Fig. 5-11

switched. The left hand for males (right for females) moves on the inside, and the right hand (left for females) moves on the outside. The movements just switch the left with the right hand. The hand positions are opposite (see Fig. 5-9). All four hand-gestures are done continuously and without stopping.

Strengthening Sphere-Shaped Divine Powers

Continuing after the fourth hand gesture, the upper hand moves on the inside with the lower hand moving on the outside. For males, the right palm gradually turns and moves down toward the chest area. The left hand for males (right for females) moves up. When both forearms have reached the chest area forming a straight line (see Fig. 5-10), pull the hands apart toward the sides

120

Fig. 5-12

(see Fig. 5-11) while turning the palms to face downward.

When both hands reach above the outside of the knees, keep the hands at the level of the waist. The forearms and the wrists are at the same level. Relax both arms (see Fig. 5-12). This position is to draw the internal divine powers out into the hands to be strengthened. They are the sphere-shaped divine powers. When strengthening the divine powers, the palms will feel warm, heavy, and numb, as if holding a weight. But do not pursue these sensations intentionally—let it happen naturally. The longer the position is held, the better. Hold until feeling too tired to endure it.

Fig. 5-13

Strengthening Pillar-Shaped Divine Powers

Following the previous position, the right hand (left for females) rotates so the palm faces upward and, at the same time, moves toward the lower abdominal area. When the hand has reached its position, the palm stays at the lower abdomen with the palm facing up. At the same time, when the right hand is moving, lift the left hand (right for females) and simultaneously move it toward the chin. With the palm still facing downward, keep the hand as high as the chin. The forearm and the hand are at the same level. At this time, both palms face each other and stay still (see Fig. 5-13). This is strengthening the pillar-shaped divine powers, such as "palm thunder," etc. Hold the position until you feel that it is impossible to hold any longer.

Fig. 5-14   Fig. 5-15

Next, the upper hand draws a semicircle in front and drops to the lower abdominal area. Simultaneously, lift the lower hand until it is right below the chin while turning the palm to face down (see Fig. 5-14). The arm is at the same level as the shoulder, with the two palms facing each other. This also strengthens the supernormal powers, only with the opposite hand positions. Hold the position until the arms become too tired to endure it.

Tranquil Cultivation

From the last position, the upper hand draws a semicircle down to the lower abdomen area. Conjoin the hands in jieyin and start the tranquil cultivation (see Fig. 5-15). Stay in Ding *(tranquil yet conscious state of mind);* the longer the better.

Fig. 5-16

Ending Position

Put the two hands together in front of the chest in heshi (see Fig. 5-16). Come out of Ding and end the cross-legged sitting.

Some Basic Requirements and Words of Caution for Practicing Falun Gong

1. The five sets of exercises of Falun Gong can be practiced consecutively or selectively. But it is usually required that you begin to practice with the first set of exercises. Moreover, it is best to do the first set of exercises three times. Of course, the other sets may still be practiced without doing the first one. Each set can be practiced individually.

2. Each movement should be carried out with accuracy and a distinct rhythm. The hands and arms should move smoothly up and down, back and forth, left and right. Following the energy mechanism, move unhurriedly, slowly, and smoothly. Do not move too fast or too slow.

3. You must keep yourself under the control of your main consciousness during practice, as Falun Gong cultivates the main consciousness. Do not deliberately seek swaying. Contain the swaying of the body when it does occur. You may open your eyes if you have to.

4. Relax the entire body, particularly the knee and hip areas. The meridians will become obstructed if you stand too rigidly.

5. During the exercises, the movements should be relaxed and natural, free and extended, easy and unencumbered. The movements should be firm yet gentle, with some force yet no rigidity or stiffness. Doing so will result in noticeable effectiveness.

6. Every time when you finish practicing, you end the movements but not the cultivation mechanism. You only need to conjoin the hands *(jieyin)*. Ending with the conjoined hands means the end of the movements. Do not put an end to the cultivation mechanism using intention, because Falun's rotation cannot be stopped.

7. Those who are weak or chronically ill may practice according to their conditions. They may practice less or choose to do any of the five sets. As to those who cannot perform movements, they may practice the lotus position sitting instead. Nonetheless, you should continue to practice.

8. There are no special requirements in terms of location, time or direction during practice. But a clean site and quiet surroundings are recommended.

9. These exercises are practiced without using any mind-intent, and you will never go awry. But do not mix Falun Gong with any other system of cultivation. Otherwise, the Falun will become deformed.

10. When you find it really impossible to enter into tranquility during practice, you may chant Master's name. As time passes, you will gradually be able to enter into the state of tranquility.

11. Some tribulations may arise when practicing. This is one way of paying for karma. Everybody has karma. When you sense discomfort in your body, do not consider it an illness. In order to eliminate your karma and pave the way for your cultivation, some tribulations may come soon and early.

12. If you cannot cross your legs for the sitting exercise, you may

first practice this set by sitting on the edge of a chair. The same effectiveness can also be achieved this way. But as a practitioner, you must be able to do the lotus position. As time progresses you will certainly be able to do it.

13. If you should see any pictures or scenes when doing the tranquil exercise, pay no attention to them and go on with your practice. If you are interfered with by some terrifying scenes or feel threatened, you should immediately remember, "I am protected by Falun Gong's Master. I am not afraid of anything." As an alternative, you may also call out the name of Master Li and continue on with your practice.

Chapter V
Questions and Answers

1. Falun and Falun Gong

Q: What does Falun consist of?

A: Falun is an intelligent being consisting of high-energy substances. It automatically transforms gong and does not exist in our dimension.

Q: What does Falun look like?

A: It can only be said that the color of Falun is golden yellow. This color does not exist in our dimension. The base color of the inner circle is a very bright red, while the base color of the outer circle is orange. There are two red-and-black taiji symbols that belong to the Tao School. There are also two other red-and-blue taiji symbols that belong to the Great Primordial-Tao School. These are two different schools. The srivatsa symbol "卍" is golden yellow. People with tianmu at a lower level see Falun rotating, similar to an electric fan. If one can see it clearly, it is very beautiful and can inspire the practitioner to cultivate even harder and strive forward vigorously.

Q: Where is Falun initially located? Where is it located later?

A: I really only give you one Falun. It is located at the lower abdomen, the same location where the dan we spoke of is cultivated and kept. Its position does not change. Some people can see many Falun spinning. Those are used externally by my Law Bodies to adjust your body.

Q: Can Falun be developed through practice and cultivation? How many of them can be developed? Is there any difference between these and the one given by master?

A: Falun can be developed through practice and cultivation. As your energy potency continues to strengthen, more and more Falun will develop. All Falun are the same. The only difference is that the Falun located at the lower abdominal area does not move around since it is the root.

Q: How can one feel and observe the presence and rotation of Falun?

A: There is no need to feel or observe it. Some people are very sensitive and will feel Falun's rotation. During the initial period after Falun is installed, you may feel a little unused to it being in your body, have abdominal pain, feel like something is moving and have the sense of warmth, and so on. After you are accustomed to it you will not have any sensation. Nonetheless, people with supernormal abilities supernormal abilities can see it. It is just the same as the stomach; you do not feel the movement of your stomach.

Q: The direction in which Falun rotates on the Falun emblem is not the same as the one on the student pass (referring to the first and second seminars in Beijing). The Falun printed on the student pass for the seminar rotates counterclockwise. Why?

A: The goal is to give you something good. Its outward emission of energy adjusts everyone's body, so it does not rotate clockwise. You can see it rotating.

Q: At what time does Master install the Falun in students?

A: We want to discuss this with all of you here. We have some students who have practiced many different practices. The difficulty lies in the fact that we have to get rid of all the messy and disorderly things that exist in the body, keeping the good and discarding the bad. This is thus an additional step. After this, Falun may be installed. According to the level of one's cultivation, the size of the Falun installed will vary. Some people have never practiced qigong before. Through their being readjusted and with their good inborn quality, some people may have their sicknesses eliminated during my class, leaving the level of qi and entering the state of the "Milky-White Body." Under those circumstances Falun can also be installed. Many people have poor health, and they will undergo constant adjustments. How can Falun be installed before the adjustments are completed? This is only the minority of people. Do not worry. I have already installed the energy mechanism that can form Falun.

Q: How is Falun carried?

A: It is not carried. I send forth Falun and install it in your lower abdomen. It is not in our physical dimension, but in a different one. With the intestines that are inside of your lower abdomen, what would happen if it started to spin and it were in this dimension? It exists in another dimension and has no conflict with this one.

Q: Will you continue to give out Falun in your next class?

A: You will get only one. Some people sense the rotation of many Falun. These are for external use, and only for the purpose of adjusting your body. The biggest feature of our exercises is that when energy is emitted, a string of Falun are being released. Before you start to practice, therefore, you already have many Falun spinning in your body and adjusting it. The Falun that I truly give to you is the one located in the lower abdomen.

Q: Does ceasing to practice mean the disappearance of Falun? How long can Falun stay in my body?

A: As long as you regard yourself as a cultivator and follow the xinxing requirements that I have discussed, when you do not practice, not only does it not disappear, but it strengthens. Your energy potency will even continue to grow. Nevertheless, if you practice more often than anyone else but fail to conduct yourself in a manner consistent with the xinxing standard I require, I am afraid that practice is a waste. Although you practice, it will not work. No matter what kind of system you practice, if you do not do it according to its requirements it is very probable that you are cultivating an evil practice. If you have only bad things on your mind, thinking, "How awful so-and-so is. I'll fix him once I develop supernormal abilities," and so on, even if you are learning Falun Gong, when you add these things into the practice and fail to follow my xinxing guidelines, aren't you practicing an evil practice as well?

Q: Master frequently says, "You cannot get Falun even if you *spend $100 million." What does it mean?*

A: It means that it is incredibly precious. What I give you is not only a Falun—there are other things [given] that guarantee your cultivation and that are also precious. None of them can be exchanged for any amount of money.

Q: Can people who came in late get Falun?

A: If you come before the last three days [of class], you can get your body adjusted and Falun—along with many other things—installed. It is hard to say if you come during the last three days, but you will still be adjusted. It is difficult to install things. Perhaps if your situation is favorable they will be installed in you.

Q: Is Falun the only thing used to rectify any incorrect condition of the human body?

A: Rectification does not entirely rely on Falun. Master also uses many other methods for correction.

Q: What is the prehistoric background of the creation of Falun Gong?

A: I think this is too broad a question and too high a level no less. Given the level we are at, it surpasses what we are entitled to know. I cannot discuss it here. But there is one thing you must understand: This is not qigong of Buddhism—it is qigong of the Buddha School. It is not Buddhism, though we have the same goal as Buddhism. It is just that we are two different cultivation methods, taking two different paths. Our goal is the same.

Q: How long is Falun Gong's history?

A: The system of practice I trained in is a little different than the system I made public. The Falun I cultivated is more powerful than what is being taught about and passed on. Also, my gong developed faster than what is permitted under this system. Nonetheless, the system of practice I have introduced to the public still permits rapid growth of gong, so cultivators' xinxing requirements are stricter and higher [than is common]. The things I have introduced to the public are rearranged and have less strict requirements [than what I practiced], but they are still stricter than an average cultivation way. Since it is different from what it originally was, I am called its founder. As to the length of Falun Gong's history, not counting the years when it was not public, you can say that it started last May (1992) when I began teaching it in the Northeast.

Q: As we listen to your lectures, what does Master give us?

A: I give everyone Falun. There is a Falun for cultivation and there are Falun for adjusting the body. At the same time, my Law bodies are taking care of you—every one of you—as long as you cultivate Falun Gong. If you do not cultivate, the Law bodies naturally will not look after you. He would not go even if he were told to. My Law bodies know clearly and precisely what you are thinking about.

Q: Can Falun Gong allow me to cultivate the Right Fruit?

A: The Great Way *(Dafa)* is without limitations. Even if you have cultivated to the level of Tathagata, it is still not the end. We are a righteous cultivation way—go ahead and cultivate! What you will attain is the Right Fruit.

2. Practice Principles and Methods

Q: After they finish "the Heavenly Circulation" and return home, some people have dreams where they clearly see themselves floating in the sky. What's that all about?

A: I can tell you all that when this kind of thing happens during your meditation or dreams, they are not dreams. It is caused by your essential spirit *(yuanshen)* leaving your physical body— something completely different from dreaming. When you dream, you do not see so clearly or in such detail. When your spirit leaves the body, what you see and how you float up can be realistically seen and remembered clearly.

Q: If Falun becomes deformed, what ill consequences will it have?

A: This signifies that one has deviated, and so Falun has lost its effectiveness. Moreover, it will bring you many problems in your cultivation. It is like your choosing not to walk on the main street, but on a side road where you get lost and cannot find your way. You will encounter problems, and these things will be reflected in daily life.

Q: When practicing by ourselves, how do we handle the home environment? Can Falun be in the house?

A: Many of you who are sitting here have already seen Falun's presence in your homes. Family members have also started to benefit from it. As we have mentioned, there exist many dimensions in the same time and at the same location. Your home is no exception, and it needs to be taken care of. The way it is generally handled it is to eliminate the bad things and then install a shield so that nothing bad can find its way in.

Q: During practice, qi hits a sick spot, making it feel painful and swollen. Why is that?

A: An sickness is a type of black energy cluster. After we break it into pieces during the early stage of the class, that spot will feel swollen. It has already lost its roots, however, and has started to discharge outward. It will be expelled very quickly, and the disease will no longer exist.

Q: My old diseases disappeared after a few days in the seminar, but suddenly reemerged a few days later. Why?

A: Because improvements take place rapidly with our cultivation system and your levels change in a very short period of time, your illness is cured before you even know it. The later symptoms are what I have discussed as the coming of "tribulations." Feel and observe carefully. They aren't the same as the symptoms of your old illness. If you look for other qigong masters to adjust your body, they will be unable to. This is a manifestation of karma during the growth of gong.

Q: While cultivating, do we still need to take medicine?

A: You should think and decide for yourself about this issue. Taking medicine during cultivation implies that you do not believe in the disease-curing effect of cultivation. If you believed in it, why would you take medicine? Yet, if you do not hold yourself up to the xinxing standard, once problems arise you will say that you have been told by Li Hongzhi not to take medicine. But Li Hongzhi has also asked you to strictly hold yourself to high xinxing standards. Have you done that? The things that exist in the bodies of true cultivators are not those of everyday people. All of the illnesses that everyday people get are not allowed to occur in your body. If, with your mind righteous and the belief that cultivation can cure illness, you discontinue your medicine, do not worry about it and do not get treatments, someone will naturally cure it for you. All of you are getting better and feeling better everyday. Why is that? My Law Bodies have been busy going back and forth to work on the bodies of many of you. They are helping you by doing these things. While cultivating, if your mind is not stable and adopts an attitude of disbelief or of "let's give it a try," then you will get nothing. Whether or not you believe in Buddhas is determined by your enlightenment quality and inborn quality. If a Buddha who could be seen clearly with human eyes were to appear here, then everyone would go to study Buddhism. The issue of transforming your thinking then would not exist. You have to first believe, then you will be able to see.

Q: Some people want to invite Teacher and Teacher's disciples to treat illness. Is this acceptable?

A: I did not come to the public to treat illness. Where there are people, there should be illness. Some people simply cannot understand the words I say, but I will not elaborate further. Practice systems of the Buddha School are for saving all sentient beings. It is acceptable to treat illness. Our treating others is organized and promotional in nature. Because I have just come to the public and am not well known, others do not recognize me and perhaps no one will attend my lectures. By curing illness during consultations, we let everyone witness Falun Gong. The results of this promotion were very good. So we did not do it entirely for the purpose of healing illness. Using powerful gong to treat illness professionally is prohibited, and neither is replacing the laws of this world with laws beyond this world permitted. Otherwise, the results of curing illness would not be good. In order to be responsible to cultivation students, we must adjust your bodies to the state where there is no longer illness—only then can you cultivate toward higher levels. If you always worry about your illness and do not actually want to cultivate in the least, even though you do not say anything, my Law body knows your thoughts clearly and you will get nothing in the end. During our class, we have already adjusted your bodies. Of course, you must first be a person who cultivates. I will not start to treat illness for you and ask for more money in the middle of a class session—we will not do that kind of thing. If your illness has not been cured, that is still an issue of your enlightenment quality. We certainly do not exclude those cases in which some individuals are very sick. The reactions may not be apparent in your body, but they are in fact quite strong. Perhaps a one-time adjustment is inadequate, yet we have already done our best. It is not that we are irresponsible; it is because the illness is simply too severe. When you go home and cultivate, we will continue to heal you until you are fully cured. These cases are very few.

Q: How do we enter tranquility when practicing? Is it considered an attachment when we think about problems at work while practicing the exercises?

A: Take matters related to self-interests lightly, and keep a clear and clean mind at all times. If you are prepared and know when tribulations will come and what they will be, then they would no longer be tribulations. Tribulations mostly come suddenly and out of nowhere. You will surely pass them if you are totally committed. Only this way can your xinxing be evaluated. Once your attachments are gone, your xinxing improved, your contending and fighting with others abandoned, your animosity and grudges forgotten, and your thinking cleaned up, then you can talk about the ability to become tranquil. If you still cannot become tranquil, then consider you, yourself to be a second person, and regard those thoughts as someone else's. However varied your thoughts are, you should step out of them and let them wander freely. There are also some people who suggest chanting the Buddha's name or counting numbers. These are all types of methods used in practices. When we practice, we are not required to focus our thoughts on something. But you have to know that you are practicing. Concerning with your problems at work, these are not considered self-interests. Those are not attachments and are of good nature. I know a monk who understands this aspect. He is the abbot of a temple and has many tasks. Yet once he sits down, he separates himself from those things. It is guaranteed that he does not think about them. This is also an ability. When he is doing the exercise, there is actually nothing on his mind— not the slightest trace of personal thoughts or ideas. If you do not mix personal things with those of work, you will still do well.

Q: What should we do when bad thoughts appear while practicing?

A: When practicing, many bad things might appear from time to time. You have just started cultivating, and it is impossible to reach a very high level at the outset; neither will we impose very high requirements on you for now. It is impractical to ask you to prevent any bad thoughts from appearing in your mind, as this has to be accomplished gradually. At the beginning it is all right, but do not let your thoughts run wild. With the passage of time, your mind will ascend, and you should hold yourself to higher standards since you are cultivating the Great Way *(Dafa)*. After you finish this class, you are no longer an everyday person. The things you now carry with you are so unique that you have to impose strict requirements on your xinxing.

Q: When I practice, I feel my head and abdomen spinning, along with discomfort in the chest area.

A: This is an initial stage caused by the rotation of Falun. You might not have this symptom in the future.

Q: What should we do when attracting small animals during practice?

A: Any kind of cultivation you practice will attract small animals. Ignore them—that's all. That is because there is a positive energy field. Particularly with the Buddha School, gong contains things that are helpful to all living beings. When our Falun revolves clockwise, it helps us; when it revolves counterclockwise, it helps others. It then rotates back and starts over again, so everything around us benefits.

Q: In the exercise, "Penetrating the Two Cosmic Extremes," is it counted as one time when the hand moves up and down once? When doing "Buddha Showing A Thousand Hands," should I imagine myself to be very big and tall before I extend my hands?

139

A: It is counted as one time after each hand moves up and down once. When doing "Buddha Showing A Thousand Hands," do not think about yourself. You will naturally feel big and tall. You only need to have a feeling that you are the largest being between heaven and earth. Just standing there is adequate. Don't always pursue that feeling intentionally, as doing so would be an attachment.

Q: When practicing the sitting meditation, what if I cannot cross my legs into the lotus position?

A: If you cannot cross your legs, you can practice by sitting on the edge of a chair. The effectiveness is the same. But since you are a cultivator, you must exercise your two legs and be able to cross them. Sit on the edge of a chair while exercising to cross your legs. You should eventually be able to cross your legs.

Q: If family members conduct themselves improperly and do not follow Zhen, Shan, and Ren, what should we do?

A: If your family members don't practice Falun Gong, this is not a problem. The main issue is cultivating yourself—cultivate yourself and don't think too much. You also have to be a little easygoing. Spend more effort on yourself.

Q: In daily life, sometimes I do wrong things and regret it afterwards, but then it happens again. Is it because my xinxing is too low?

A: Since you can write about it [in your question], it proves that you have already improved your xinxing and are able to acknowledge your wrongdoing. Everyday people are oblivious when they have done wrong. This means that you have already surpassed everyday people. You did wrong the first time and did not guard your xinxing. It is a process. The next time you encounter a problem, try again to improve.

Q: Can people in their forties or fifties reach the state of "three flowers gathering above one's head"?

A: Because we cultivate both mind and body, age does not matter. As long as you focus on cultivation and can follow the xinxing guidelines as I've illustrated them, the phenomenon of prolonging one's life will appear as you cultivate. Doesn't this give you enough time to cultivate? Yet there is one thing pertaining to exercises that cultivate both mind and body: If, when your life is extended, there is a problem with your xinxing, your life will immediately be in danger. Because your life is prolonged for the purpose of cultivation, once your xinxing deviates, your life will immediately be in danger.

Q: How should we handle the degree of strength to achieve the effect of "strong yet gentle"?

A: This has to be explored by you, yourself. For example, when we do large hand gestures the hands look very soft, but the gestures are actually done with strength. The force is quite strong between the forearm, wrist, and among the fingers. Meanwhile, however, they all appear very soft. This is "strength within gentleness." When I performed the hand gestures for all of you, I gave it to you already. Gradually observe and feel it during your practice.

Q: Is it true that sexual relations between men and women are unnecessary? Should young people divorce?

A: The issue of sexual desire was discussed previously. At your current level, you are not asked to become a monk or nun. It is you who are asking yourself to be one, [not us]. The key is for you to abandon that attachment [to sexual desire]. You have to abandon all of the attachments that you do not want to abandon. To an everyday person, this is one kind of desire. As to cultivators, we have to be able to let it go and not attach importance to it. Some people actually pursue this, and their minds are filled with these things. They have too much desire, even for everyday people. It is even more inappropriate for cultivators. Because you cultivate and family members do not, it is permissible at your current stage to lead a normal life. When reaching a higher level, you will know for yourself what to do.

Q: Is it all right to fall asleep when sitting in meditation? How should I handle it? I sometimes lose awareness for as long as three minutes and don't know what's going on.

A: No, it's not all right to fall asleep. How can you sleep when you practice? Sleeping in meditation is also a form of demonic interference. The matter of dozing off should not occur. Could it be that you didn't express your question clearly in writing? Losing awareness for three minutes doesn't mean that something has gone wrong. The state of losing awareness frequently happens to people with a superior ability for attaining Ding *(tranquil yet conscious state of mind)*. Nonetheless, it will be problematic if it continues for a long time.

Q: Is it true that anyone who is determined to attain the Right

Fruit through cultivation can attain it? What if their inborn quality is inferior?

A: It all depends on what kind of determination you have—the critical factor is how determined you are. As to people with inferior inborn quality, it still depends on your determination and enlightenment quality.

Q: Can I practice when I have a cold or fever?

A: I'm telling you that after you finish this class, you will never get sick. You might not believe it. Why do my students sometimes have symptoms similar to having a cold or a fever? That is the passing of a tribulation and hardship, and it implies that improving to another level is due. They all understand that they don't need to pay attention to it, and it will pass.

Q: Can pregnant women practice Falun Gong?

A: It's not a problem, because Falun is installed in another dimension. There are no vigorous movements in our practice system that could negatively impact a pregnant woman. It is actually beneficial to them.

Q: When Teacher is away from us, will there be any spatial distance?

A: Many people have this kind of thought: "Teacher is not in Beijing. What should we do?" It's the same when you practice other types of exercises—the teachers cannot watch over you everyday. The Law *(Fa)* has been taught to you; principles have been taught to you. This set of exercises has been taught to you;

a complete set of things has been given to you. How you cultivate is completely in your hands. You cannot say that you would have a guarantee were you by my side, and that you don't if you are not. Let's give an example. More than two thousand years since Sakyamuni passed away, those Buddhists still continue in their cultivation without second thoughts. So whether or not you cultivate is a personal issue.

Q: Will practicing Falun Gong result in bigu?[69]

A: No, it will not, because *bigu* is a cultivation method of the Great Primordial-Tao School way of cultivation that existed even before Buddhism or Taoism; it existed prior to the establishment of religions. This method often belongs to solitary cultivation. Since in the time of the Great Primordial-Tao School there was no monk or temple system, they had to cultivate halfway up a mountain, where no one could supply them with food. When they had to cultivate in seclusion, which required remaining still for six months to a year, they adopted this approach. Today, our cultivation doesn't need bigu since it is a method used under special circumstances. It is certainly not a supernormal ability. Some people teach this method. I say that if all people the whole world over did not need to eat, it would disrupt the social conditions of everyday people. So it would be a problem. If no one ate, would that be a human society? That's not permitted, and it shouldn't be that way.

Q: To what level can these five sets of exercises lead us?

---

[69] *bigu* (bee-goo)— "no grain"; an ancient term for abstinence from food and water.

A: These five sets will allow you to cultivate to an extremely high level. Certainly, you will know which level you want to cultivate to when the time comes. Since there is no limit to gong, you will have another predestined arrangement when you have reached that point, and you will obtain the Great Way *(Dafa)* at an even higher level.

Q: "The Fa refines the practitioner." Does it mean that since Falun always rotates we don't need to practice?

A: Practicing is different from cultivation in temples. In fact, when you cultivate in a temple, you actually have to sit in meditation too; that is an ability that needs to be practiced. You cannot say you just want to develop your gong and have it grow atop your head without doing any practice—how could you be called a practitioner? Every school has its own set of inherited things that need to be developed via practice.

Q: Practitioners of other cultivation systems claim, "Practices that don't use mind-intent are not cultivation." Is this correct?

A: There are so many different remarks, but no one has disclosed the Great Way *(Dafa)* to you as I have. The Buddha School believes that a cultivation method that uses intention cannot be of a very high level; a "cultivation method that uses intention" does not refer to practice that have movements. Their meditation and hand conjoining *(jieyin)* are also movements, so the size or number of movements is not the concern. "Intention" and "non-intention" *(wuwei)* refer to your mind-intent. In terms of pursuits, if you pursue and have intention, those are attachments. That is what it means.

Q: Xinxing is not equivalent to de. You say that de determines one's level, but you then say that the level of xinxing determines the level of gong. Are these statements contradictory?

A: You may not have heard it clearly. Xinxing covers a broad range of things, with de being a part of it. It also includes forbearance, the ability to bear sufferings, enlightenment quality, how you deal with conflicts, etc. All of these are issues of xinxing that also include the transformation of gong and de. This is a broad matter. How much de you have does not indicate how much gong you possess. Instead, it indicates how much your gong can develop in the future. Only through the improvement of xinxing can de be transformed into gong.

Q: Each family member practices a different type of qigong. Will they interfere with one another?

A: No, not with Falun Gong. But I don't know whether other practice systems will interfere with one another. As for our Falun Gong, no one can interfere with it. Also, you will be beneficial to your family members because we cultivate the righteous way and will not go awry.

Q: There are many different statements prevailing in society, such as those of chain letters. How are we supposed to deal with them?

A: I will tell you that these things are pure deceit. Don't return his letter—how pathetic it is. You don't have to deal with it. You can discern whether or not this is righteous simply by taking a look at it. Our Fa has strict requirements for xinxing cultivation. I call some qigong masters "qigong merchants," as they use qigong as a form of merchandise, turning it into an asset to exchange for money. These kinds of people have nothing real to teach. If they do possess a little bit of something, it won't be of a high level. Some of it may even be evil.

Q: If Falun Gong students have been formally converted to Buddhism in temples, what should they do? Should they withdraw?

A: This has little to do with us. Although you've already been formally converted to Buddhism, that is only a formality.

Q: There are several of us whose heads have been feeling swollen and dizzy since we began our study.

A: This might be because you are new students whose bodies haven't been fully adjusted. The energy I emit is very powerful. When the ill qi comes out, it will make your head feel bloated. This happens when we're treating the illness in your head, and it is a good thing. But the quicker your illness goes away, the stronger the reaction. When we held seven-day seminars, some people couldn't take it. Problems could arise if the time were to be shortened even more. The emitted energy is very powerful, and the reactions are very strong, with the head feeling unbearably bloated. It seems that a ten-day seminar is safer. People who came in late may react a little stronger.

Q: Can we smoke cigarettes or drink during cultivation? What if we have to drink due to the nature of our work?

A: This is how I view the subject. Our Buddha School qigong prohibits drinking. After going a while without drinking, perhaps you will want to drink again. Quit gradually, but don't take too long, or otherwise you will be punished. As to smoking, I think it's an issue of willpower. As long as you want to quit, you can. Everyday people often think, "I'll quit smoking today." Several days later, they cannot adhere to it. Then, after a couple of days, they take up that thought again and try to quit one more time. Going about things this way, they are never able to quit smoking. Everyday people live in this world, and having social interactions when in contact with others is unavoidable. But, having already started cultivating, you should no longer consider yourself an everyday person. As long as you have the will, you will achieve your goal. Of course, some of my students still smoke cigarettes. He can quit on his own, but when someone else hands him one he is too polite to refuse. He wants to smoke, and he feels uncomfortable when going a couple of days without smoking. But if he smokes again, he will feel uncomfortable. You must exercise control over yourself. Some people are in the public relations business, and this demands that they frequently wine and dine guests. This is a difficult problem to solve. Do your best to drink as little as possible, or think of another way to solve this problem.

Q: When we still cannot see Falun spinning, if we think of it spinning clockwise, will we affect the Falun that happens to be spinning counterclockwise?

A: Falun spins automatically. It doesn't need the guidance of your mind-intent. I want to emphasize it one more time: Do not use intention. Actually, intentions cannot control it anyway. Don't think that you can use your intention to force it to rotate in the opposite direction. The Falun located in the lower abdomen is not controlled by intention. The Falun that are used externally to adjust your body might accept your intention if you wish to have them rotate in a particular way; you may sense that. I tell you: Do not do this. With intention, you are unable to practice. Won't practicing with intention turn into "the practitioner refines gong"? It should be the Falun or Law *(Fa)* that refines the practitioner. Why is it that you can never loosen your grip on your intentions? Any cultivation that has reached a high level—even Taoist cultivation—is not guided by intention.

Q: What is the best time, location, and direction to practice Falun Gong so that the best results can be achieved? How many times a day is considered appropriate? Does it matter if one practices before or after meals?

A: Because Falun is round and a miniature of this universe, it cultivates the principles of the universe. Moreover, the universe is in motion, so it is the Law *(Fa)* that refines the practitioner. When you are not cultivating, it cultivates you, and this is different from any other cultivation principle or theory that has been made public. Mine is the only system where "the Fa refines the practitioner." All other cultivation methods take the path of dan, unlike ours, and intentionally cultivate gong and maintain dan. Our system can be practiced anytime, for when you don't practice the gong cultivates you. There is no need to choose a time. Practice as much as you can, according to how much time you have. Our exercises don't have a very strict requirement with this, but we do have strict requirements for xinxing. Our exercises are not concerned with direction, either. Whichever direction you choose to face is all right, because the universe is revolving and in motion. If you face the west, it's not necessarily the real west. If you face the east, it's not necessarily the real east. I have asked my students to face west when practicing just to show respect. It does not, in fact, have any impact. You can exercise at any location, inside or outside of your home. But I still feel that we should find a place with relatively good ground, surroundings, and air. Particularly, it should be far away from dirty things such as garbage cans or toilets. Nothing else really matters. The Great Way's cultivation is not concerned with time, location, or direction. You can exercise before or after meals, but if you are too full it will be uncomfortable to practice right away. It is better to rest a little while. When you are so hungry that your stomach is rumbling, it will also be hard for you to become tranquil. You should manage this based on your own situation.

Q: Is there any requirement after the exercises are finished, such as rubbing the face?

A: We don't worry about cold water or other things after the exercises, and neither do we need to rub the face or hands. These are all intended to open the meridians and acupuncture points in human body at the initial stage. We cultivate the Great Way *(Dafa)*, which does not involve these things. Right now you are not in the state where your body has just been adjusted. It seems very, very difficult for an everyday person to start becoming a cultivator, and some forms of [qigong] exercises cannot directly change the human body. Some of their requirements are very complicated. We don't have those here, and neither do we have those kinds of concepts. Don't bother with what I have not talked about—just keep on cultivating. Since we cultivate the Great Way, within a matter of days your body will pass through the initial state in which it fears this and that or the process in which it needs this or that requirement. I would not state that it's equivalent to a few years of practice with other cultivation methods, but it is almost the same. I don't talk about things at lower levels, such as this direction, that meridian, etc. We only discuss things of a higher level. The cultivation of the Great Way is true cultivation. It is cultivation, not exercises.

Q: Can we use the bathroom right after we're finished with our exercises? There are lots of bubbles in my urine. Is qi leaking out?

A: That's not a problem. Since we cultivate at higher levels, our urine or excrement does indeed contain energy. Nevertheless, it has only a very small amount and it does not impact anything. Cultivating the Great Way also means the salvation of all sentient beings. This little leakage is no big deal, as what we gain back is much more. The energy I have discharged in teaching this class is immensely powerful, and it remains all over the walls.

Q: Can we spread and promote Falun Gong? Can we teach it to people who didn't attend the class? Can people who haven't attended the class practice at the assistance center? Is it all right to mail audio tapes and books to relatives or friends living out of town?

A: One won't go awry when spreading our cultivation system and letting more people benefit from it. I've lectured to you on many Laws *(Fa),* letting you know the Law of higher levels and letting you understand and see things of a higher level. I've told you all of these in advance since I fear that if I wait, you won't understand when you see or encounter these things. You can teach other people to practice, but you are unable to install Falun. What should you do? I've said that my Law Bodies *(fashen)* will leave you if you cultivate on and off and don't really practice. If you truly cultivate, the Law Bodies will look after you. So when you teach someone, you bring the information I taught to you; it carries the Falun-forming energy mechanism. If the person you teach puts effort into practicing, Falun will form. If he is predestined and has good inborn quality, he can get Falun right on the spot. Our book is very detailed. Good cultivation can still take place without being taught by someone directly.

Q: Is Falun Gong concerned with breathing? How do we regulate breaths?

A: You don't need to regulate your breath when cultivating Falun Gong. We aren't concerned with breathing. That's what one would learn at the entry level. We don't need it here, because regulating and controlling breathing is for cultivating dan, whereby one adds air and feeds the fire.[70] Breathing in an upstream or downstream style, or swallowing saliva, are each for the purpose of cultivating dan. We don't cultivate that way. Everything you need is accomplished by Falun. The more difficult and higher level things are done by Master's Law Body. Actually, no cultivation method—even including the Taoist school ones in which cultivation of dan is discussed in more detail—is accomplished by means of intention. As a matter of fact, it is the grand master of that particular school who helps one cultivate and transform those things, and this is done without one's knowledge. You can't possibly accomplish it on your own deliberately, unless you have reached enlightenment. Only the enlightened can do it.

Q: Do we need to use mind focusing when practicing? Where does one's attention lie in these exercises lie?

---

[70] A Taoist metaphor for the process of internal alchemy.

A: We don't use mind focusing here. I have been telling everyone not to use mind focusing, and to give up their attachments. Do not seek to use any kind of mind-intend. In the third set, where the two palms carry qi to penetrate the two cosmic extremes, all that is needed is one quick thought. Don't think about anything else.

Q: Is collecting energy the same as collecting qi?

A: What do we collect qi for? What we cultivate is the Great Way *(Dafa)*. In the future, you won't even be able to emit qi. What we cultivate is not qi, which is at a lower level. We emit light instead, and energy collection is done by Falun, not by ourselves. Yet the exercise, "Penetrating the Two Cosmic Extremes," for instance, is actually used to open up your body. It can also function to collect energy, but that's not the main purpose. How does one collect qi? Since you cultivate the Great Way *(Dafa)*, with the simple wave of your hand you will feel heaviness above your head, as a great deal of qi has come. But what do you need it for? Energy doesn't need to be collected deliberately.

Q: Does Falun Gong cover "building a foundation within one hundred days" and "fetal breathing"?

A: Those are all practices of lower levels, and we don't cultivate them. We have long passed those unstable entry-level stages.

Q: Is Falun Gong concerned with the balance of yin and yang?

A: These are at the level of cultivating qi—things of a lower level. When you go beyond that level, the issue of balance between yin and yang doesn't exist in your body anymore. It doesn't matter which system you cultivate: As long as you receive genuine teaching from a master, you are guaranteed to depart from the lower level. You will have to completely discard everything you learned in the past, keeping nothing. A new set of things will be cultivated at the new level. After passing this new level, another new set of things will be cultivated again. It's like this.

Q: Can we practice when it thunders? Do practitioners of Falun Gong fear sound?

A: Let me give you an example. I once taught students in the courtyard of a large building in Beijing. It was going to rain, and the thunder was extremely intense. At that time they were practicing exercises that were taught only to disciples, and these required doing a walking moving-stance on Falun. I saw the rain coming, yet they were not finished with the exercise. The heavy rain, however, could not manage to fall. The clouds were sitting very low, rolling over the top of the building. With the thunder crashing and booming, it was very dark. At that time a thunderbolt struck the edge of the Falun, but we weren't harmed—not even a hair was. We could see clearly how the thunderbolt had struck the ground and left us still unharmed. This means that our gong gives us protection. When I practice, I usually don't care what the weather is. Whenever I think of practicing, I practice. As long as there is time, I will practice. I'm not afraid of sound, either. Other methods fear sound, because when you are very, very tranquil and suddenly hear a very loud sound, it will feel to you as if the qi all over your body was going to explode, flickering and running outside the body. But don't worry, our cultivation does not go awry. Of course, do your best to find a quiet place to practice.

Q: Should we visualize Master's image?

A: There is no need to visualize. When your tianmu is open you will see my Law Body next to you.

Q: Is there any requirement when practicing these five sets of exercises? Must they be practiced all together? Can we count silently when practicing those that require nine repetitions? Will it be counterproductive if we do more than nine repetitions or remember certain movements incorrectly?

A: You can practice any set among the five sets of exercises. I think it's best to practice the first set prior to doing the others, because the first set opens up the entire body. You should practice it once first. After your body is fully opened, proceed to the other sets; this is more effective. Practice as much as you can, according to how much time you have available. You may also opt to select a particular set to practice. The movements in the third and fourth sets should be repeated nine times respectively, and it's written in the book that you can count silently. You can go home and try asking your child to stand nearby and count while you practice. When you are finished doing the nine repetitions, you will no longer find the energy mechanism needed to continue repetitions since that is how my things work. At the beginning you need to think about it, but once you have gotten into the habit you will stop naturally. If you remember some movements incorrectly or do too many or too few repetitions, correct them and it should be fine.

Q: Why is the end of the movements not the end of the practice?

A: Falun revolves automatically, and it knows instantly that you've stopped practicing. It contains a tremendous amount of energy and can instantly take back what it has emitted much better than what your intentionally doing so could. This isn't the end of the practice; rather, it is taking back the energy. Other cultivation methods actually do end the minute their exercises are over. Our system is being practiced at all times—even when the movements are stopped, so the practice cannot be terminated. Even if you want to stop Falun's revolving, you will be unable. If I discuss it at a deeper level you won't understand. If you could stop its rotation, I would have to stop, too. Will you be able to stop me?

Q: Can we practice jieyin (conjoining the hands) and heshi (pressing the hands together before the chest) as a standing stance exercise?

A: The first set, Buddha Showing a Thousand Hands, cannot be practiced as a standing stance exercise. When you use too much strength to stretch, you will encounter problems.

Q: Is it required that the underarms be kept hollow during practice? When practicing the first set, my underarms feel very tense. What is happening?

A: Do you have sickness? During the initial stage, when adjustments are being made to your body you may discover various phenomena. You will have some symptoms, but they are not evoked by the exercises.

Q: Can people who haven't attend Teacher Li's classes practice together with other students in the parks?

A: Yes. Any student can teach others how to practice. When students teach the exercises to others, it's not in the manner I have been teaching you here—I directly adjust your bodies. But there are still people who acquire Falun as soon as they start practicing, because behind every student exists my Law Body; it can directly take care of these matters. This all depends on people's predestined relationship. When their predestined relationship is strong, they can get Falun right on the spot; if your predestined relationship is not as strong, you can, through long-term practice, develop the revolving mechanism yourself. Through more practice, you will manage to evolve the revolving mechanism into a Falun.

Q: What's the meaning of the hand gestures in the tranquil exercise, Strengthening Divine Powers?

A: Our language cannot explain it. Each gesture embodies a wealth of meaning. In general, they say: "I will start practicing the movements and practicing the Buddha's Fa. I will adjust my body and enter into a cultivation state."

Q: When we reach the state of the Milk-White Body through cultivation, is it true that all the sweat pores have been opened and body-breathing is formed?

A: Try to feel it everyone: you have already passed this level. In order to adjust your bodies to the state of the Milk-White Body, I had to lecture on Fa for more than ten hours, and no less. We immediately bring you to a state that would take decades or longer to reach were you practicing other cultivation methods. Because this step does not require xinxing standards, it is done according to the mater's ability. Before you've even sensed it, that level has

157

already been passed. Perhaps it was only a few hours long. One day you might feel very sensitive, but in a short while you are not as sensitive. In fact, a major level was just passed. With other cultivation methods, however, you would remain in this state for a year or more; those are actually at a lower level.

Q: Is it all right if we think about all the movements of Falun Gong while riding the bus or waiting in line?

A: Our exercises require neither mind-intent nor some specific length of time for daily practice. Undoubtedly, the longer you practice the better. When you don't practice, the practice refines you instead. But during the initial stage it's better to practice more, strengthening it. Some students find that when they go on business trips for a couple of months, they have no time to practice. Yet this is without impact at all. Falun still revolves after they return since it never stops. As long as in your heart you consider yourself a cultivator and you guard your xinxing well, it will continue to function. But there is one thing: If you don't practice and you mix yourself with everyday people, it will dissolve.

Q: Can Falun Gong and Tantrism be practiced together?

A: Tantrism also uses a Law Wheel *(Falun)*, but it cannot be practiced together with our cultivation method. If you have cultivated Tantrism and its Law Wheel has already been formed, you can continue to cultivate Tantrism because Tantrism is also a righteous cultivation way. Yet they cannot be practiced at the same time. The Law Wheel of Tantrism cultivates the central meridian and revolves horizontally. Its Law Wheel differs from our Falun, and has mantras on the wheel. Our Falun is placed vertically on the lower abdomen with the flat side facing out. With space on the abdomen being limited, my Falun by itself already completely covers the area. If one more is placed there, things will be messed up.

Q: Can we practice other Buddha School cultivation systems while practicing Falun Gong? Can we listen to audio tapes that chant Bodhisattva Avalokitesvara's name? Can lay Buddhists who live at home chant scriptures after they have learned Falun Gong? Can we practice other exercises at the same time?

A: I think not. Every method is a way of cultivation. If you truly want to cultivate and not just cure diseases or improve health, you must cultivate only one way. This is a serious matter. Cultivating toward higher levels requires that one keeps cultivating in one cultivation way. This is an absolute truth. Even the cultivation ways within the Buddha School cannot be mixed. The cultivation we talk about is of higher levels and inherited from many, many ages ago. Practicing according to what you sense is haphazard. Looking from a different dimension, the transformation process is extremely profound and complex. Just as with a precision instrument, if you remove one of its components and replace it with something else, it will break down immediately. The same goes for cultivation: nothing should be mixed in. It's bound to go wrong if you intermingle it. It's the same for all cultivation ways: If you want to cultivate, you must focus on only one way. You won't be able to cultivate whatsoever if you do otherwise. The saying, "gathering the best of every school," is only applicable to the level of healing diseases and improving health. It won't bring you to higher levels.

Q: Will we interfere with each other when practicing with people who practice other cultivation ways?

A: Regardless of what kind of cultivation way he practices—from the Tao School, a supernormal practice, or one of the Buddha School—as long as it's righteous, it has no impact on us at all. You will not interfere with him either. It is beneficial to him if he practices near you. Because Falun is an intelligent being and it doesn't cultivate dan, it will automatically help.

Q: Can we ask other qigong masters to adjust our bodies? Will it have any impact if we listen to lectures by other qigong masters?

A: I believe that after this class you will sense what state your body has reached. After a while, it's not permissible for you to have sickness. When problems do come again, they may feel like having a cold or stomachache, but they are actually no longer the same. They are instead tribulations and tests. If you look for other qigong masters, it means that you don't comprehend or believe what I have said. With the mentality of pursuit, you will attract evil messages that will interfere with your cultivation. If the gong of that qigong master comes from futi, you might also end up attracting those beings. The same thing goes for listening to the lectures: doesn't "the desire to listen" mean you pursue something? You have to comprehend this issue on your own. This is an issue of xinxing, and I'm not going to step in. If he talks about very high-level principles or xinxing matters, it might be all right. You attended my class, and through great effort your body has been adjusted. Originally, the messages from other practices in your body were very scrambled, messing up the body. Everything has now been adjusted to the best state, with the bad removed and the good retained. Of course, I don't object to you learning other cultivation methods. If you feel Falun Gong isn't good, you can learn other cultivation methods. But I hold that if you learn too many different things, it's not good for you. You have already cultivated the Great Law *(Dafa)* and Law Bodies are right by your side. You've acquired things of a higher level and now you want to go back and search again!

Q: If we practice Falun Gong, can we study other methods, such as massage, self-defense, Single-Finger Zen, taiji, etc.? If we don't practice these but just read related books, will it have any impact?

A: It's all right to study massage and self-defense, but when cruelty comes to you, you will feel uncomfortable. Single-Finger Zen and taiji are classified as qigong. If you practice those you will be adding things, making impure the substances of mine that exist in your body. If you read the books that talk about xinxing, it is all right. But some authors draw conclusions even before they've figured it all out themselves. It will confuse your thoughts.

Q: When doing "Holding the Wheel in Front of the Head," my hands will touch at times. Is it all right?

A: Do not let the hands touch. We require you to keep a small gap. If the hands touch, the energy on the hands will return back into the body.

Q: When practicing the second set, if we can't hold the arms anymore, can we put them down and then continue with the practice?

A: Cultivation is very bitter. It's not effective if the minute you feel sore you bring them down. The guideline is this: the longer the better. But you should go according to your own ability.

Q: In the full-lotus position, why is the left leg underneath the right one for females?

A: This is because our cultivation takes into consideration one essential factor: The female body is different from the male body. So cultivation should match the female physique if she wants to use her benti to transform herself. For women, it is usually the left leg that supports the right, conforming to her own situation. Men are the opposite, as the essential nature is different.

Q: Is listening to tapes or music or reciting verse acceptable when practicing?

A: If it's decent Buddha School music, you can listen. Yet genuine cultivation needs no music since it requires the ability to enter tranquility. Listening to music is an attempt to replace various thoughts with just one.

Q: When practicing Penetrating the Two Cosmic Extremes, should we relax or use strength?

A: Penetrating the Two Cosmic Extremes requires standing naturally and relaxed, unlike the first set. All of the other exercises require that you relax; this is different from the first set.

3. Cultivating Xinxing

Q: I want to be up to the standards of Zhen, Shan, and Ren. But yesterday I dreamed that I was arguing very bitterly with someone, and when I wanted to forbear I failed. Was that supposed to help me improve my xinxing?

A: It certainly was. I have already told you what dreams are. You should try to think about it and understand it yourself. The things that will help you improve your xinxing come suddenly and unexpectedly. They don't wait until you're mentally prepared to welcome them. To judge whether a person is good or bad, you can only test him when he's not mentally prepared.

Q: Does the "Ren" of Zhen, Shan, and Ren in Falun Gong mean that we should tolerate everything, regardless of whether it is correct or not?

A: The "Ren" I talk about refers to improving xinxing on the issues related to your own self-interest and all those attachments that you've been unwilling to abandon. In fact, "Ren" isn't an awful thing, even to everyday people. Let me tell you a story. Han Xin was a great senior general who had loved martial arts since he was young. During his time, people who were learning martial arts liked to carry around swords. When Han Xin was walking in the street, a ruffian came toward him and challenged him: "What are you carrying that sword for? Do you dare to kill people? If you do, kill me first." As he was talking, he stuck out his neck. He said, "If you don't dare to kill me, crawl between my legs!" Han Xin then crawled between his legs. He had an excellent ability of "Ren." Some people consider forbearance weakness, as though one is easily bullied. The truth of the matter is that people who can practice forbearance have a very strong will. As to the right or wrong of matters, you must look to see if they really conform to the principle of the universe. You may

163

think that you're not at fault for a particular incident, and that it's the other person who has upset you. In fact, you don't really know why. You will say, "I know, it's just about something trivial." What I say is a different principle that can't be seen in this material dimension. To put the matter jokingly, perhaps you owed others in your previous life. How can you judge its right or wrong? We have to forbear. How can you upset and offend others first and then forbear? Toward those people who have really upset you, you should not only forbear, but also be grateful. If a person yells at you and then blames you for the matter in front of your teacher, accusing you of yelling at him, you should say "thank you" in your heart. You say, "Wouldn't I turn into Ah Q?" That's your opinion. If you don't deal with this incident the same way he does, you have improved your xinxing. He gains in this material dimension, but he gives things away to you in another dimension, doesn't he? Your xinxing has been improved and the black substance transformed. You've gained in three ways. Why not be thankful to him? It's not easy to comprehend from the standpoint of everyday people, but I'm not lecturing to everyday people. I am lecturing to cultivators.

Q: People without futi can improve xinxing to avoid having futi. What if one already has futi? How can he get rid of it?

A: One righteous thought will subdue a hundred evils. You received the Great Law *(Dafa)* today. From now on, even if futi brings you benefits, you should not accept it. When it brings you money, fame, and personal gain, you feel very happy inside your heart, thinking, "See how capable I am," and you show off in front of others. When you do feel uncomfortable, you don't want to live with it and look for Teacher to treat you. How come you don't behave yourself when it keeps giving you good things? We

164

can't take care of it for you, because you have accepted all the benefits it has brought you. It's unacceptable if all you want to have is benefit. It will become fearful only when you don't want it—even the good things it brings, when you continue to cultivate according to the method taught by Teacher, and when you have become righteous and your mind is firm. If you reject it further when it tries to give you some benefits, it's time for it to leave. If it stays on you, it will be committing a wrong deed. At that point I can take care of it. It will disappear with a simple wave of my hand. But it won't work if you want to have the benefits it brings you.

Q: Will people acquire futi by practicing in the park?

A: I have explained it to you many times. We cultivate a righteous way. If your mind is righteous, all kinds of evil things will be subdued. In cultivation of a righteous way the mind is very pure and upright, so nothing can approach the practitioner. Falun is something incredible. Not only are evil things unable to attach themselves to you—they have fear when near you. If you don't believe it, you can practice at other places. They all fear you. If I tell you the number of futi [out there], all of you will be scared; many people have futi. After these people have reached the goal of healing diseases and improving health, they continue to practice. What do they want? These problems will occur when their minds are not righteous. Yet blame shouldn't be placed on these people, as they don't understand the principles. One of the goals of my coming to the public is to help correct these wrong things for you.

Q: What supernormal abilities will one develop in the future?

A: I don't want to talk about this. Because each individual has his own set of conditions, it's very difficult to say. Different supernormal abilities will be developed at different levels. The critical factor is your xinxing at each level. If attachments have been abandoned in certain regard, a supernormal ability may be developed in that regard. But that supernormal ability has to be in its early stage and so it won't be very powerful. When your xinxing hasn't reached a very high level, supernormal abilities cannot be given to you. Yet in our class some individuals have pretty good inborn quality. They have developed a supernormal walking ability that shields them from rain. Some have also developed the supernormal ability of teleportation.

Q: Does "cultivating xinxing" or "getting rid of all attachments" refer to the Buddha School's "emptiness" and the Tao School's "nothingness"?

A: The "xinxing" or "de" we talk about isn't contained in the "emptiness" of the Buddha School or "nothingness" of the Tao School. Rather, the emptiness of the Buddha School and nothingness of the Tao School are included in our "xinxing."

Q: Will a Buddha always remain a Buddha?

A: After you've reached enlightenment through cultivation, you are an enlightened being—that is, a being of higher levels. But there's no guarantee that you will never misbehave. Of course, normally you won't commit wrongdoing at that level since you have seen the truth. But if you've handled yourself poorly, you will drop down without exception. If you always do good things, you will stay up there forever.

166

Q: What is a person with "great inborn quality"?

A: This is determined by a few factors: 1. good inborn quality; 2. outstanding enlightenment quality; 3. excellent ability of forbearance; 4. few attachments, while taking matters of this world lightly. These are people with great inborn quality, who are very hard to find.

Q: Can people without good inborn quality develop gong if they practice Falun Gong?

A: People without good inborn quality can also develop gong, because everyone carries some amount of de. It's impossible not to have any de at all—there's no one like that. Even if you don't have the white substance on you, you still have the black substance. Through cultivation, the black substance can be transformed into the white substance; this is just one extra step. When you have suffered during cultivation, improved your xinxing, and made sacrifices, you have developed gong. Cultivation is the prerequisite. It's the master's Law Body who transforms it into gong.

Q: When one is born, his entire life has already been arranged. Does hard work make any difference?

A: Of course it does. Your hard work is also something that's been arranged, so you can't help but work hard. You are an everyday person. Things of much significance, however, cannot be changed.

167

Q: When the tianmu hasn't been opened, how do we tell whether the messages we receive are good or bad?

A: It's difficult to do so on your own. Throughout your cultivation process exist many problems that put your xinxing to the test. The protection extended to you by my Law Body is to prevent endangerment of your life. The Law Body, however, might not take care of certain problems that need to be overcome, resolved, and comprehended by you. Sometimes when evil messages come, perhaps they will tell you what the lotto numbers are, but the numbers might be right or wrong. Or they could also tell you other things. It's all up to you. When your mind is upright, evil things cannot invade. There shouldn't be any problem as long as you guard your xinxing well.

Q: Can we practice when we feel emotionally upset?

A: When you're in a bad mood it is difficult for you to sit down and become tranquil. You will have thoughts of bad things running wild in your mind. Messages exist in cultivation. When bad thoughts are on your mind, these things will enter into your cultivation, turning it into an evil way's purposive cultivation. The exercises you practice may have been taught to you by Yan Xin,[71] by some other master, or by a living Buddha of Tantrism. But if you didn't strictly follow their xinxing requirements, what you practiced was not their cultivation way—even though they were the ones who taught you. Let's all think about it: if you're practicing the standing stance and feeling very tired while your mind is still very active, thinking, "Why is so-and-so in my company so nasty? Why did he report me? What can I do to get a raise? Prices are rising—I should do more shopping," then aren't

---

[71] Yan Xin—a well-known qigong master in China.

you purposefully, subconsciously, and unknowingly cultivating an evil way? So if you are experiencing emotional trouble, it's best not to practice then.

Q: What is the standard for "extremely high xinxing"?

A: Xinxing comes through cultivation and doesn't have any set standards. It is all left for you to comprehend. If you insist that xinxing has standards, then it is that when you encounter incidents, you should try to think, "If it was an enlightened person who was faced with this, what would he do?" Exemplary people are outstanding, of course, but they are still models for everyday people.

Q: We shouldn't hold a suspicious attitude toward talks or speeches delivered by other qigong masters. But when we run into con-artists who deceive people for money, what should we do?

A: That doesn't have to be the case. You should first take a look at what they discuss, and then judge on your own whether it's deceitful. To judge whether or not a qigong master is decent, you can look at his xinxing. Gong is always as high as xinxing.

Q: How do we eliminate karma or, as Buddhism calls it, "karmic debt"?

A: Cultivation is itself a form of eliminating karma. The best way is to improve your xinxing, as this enables the black substance's transformation into the white substance, de. De is then transformed into gong.

Q: If we practice Falun Gong, are there any precepts that forbid us to do certain things?

A: The majority of what's prohibited in Buddhism cannot be done by us, but we have a different perspective. We are not monks or nuns. We live among everyday people, so it is different. If you take some things lightly, it will suffice. Certainly, as your energy potency continues to grow and reach very high levels, what will be required of your xinxing will be very high, too.

4. Tianmu

Q: When master was lecturing, I saw a three-foot golden halo above master's head, and many golden halos the size of the head behind your back.

A: The tianmu of this person has already reached a pretty high level.

Q: I saw golden light mixed in the wine spit out by master's disciples when they were giving treatments to other people.

A: I say this person has cultivated pretty well. He could see the supernormal abilities that were emitted.

Q: Will it have any impact on a child if his tianmu is opened? Does an open tianmu release energy?

A: It's very easy for children under the age of six to have their tianmu opened. If small children don't practice, the opening of their tianmu will result in leakage of energy; however, someone in the family must practice. It's best to have him look through his tianmu once a day, preventing it from being closed as well as preventing too much leakage. It's best for small children themselves to practice cultivation. The more they use it, the more energy will leak out. What it impacts isn't their physical body, but their most fundamental things. But if it's well preserved, it won't have any impact. What I just talked about refers to small children, not adults. Some people have tianmu that are wide open and they are unafraid of leaking energy, yet they cannot see things that are at a very high level. There are also some who can see very high levels. When they see, a Law Body or other master provides the energy. It's not a problem.

Q: I saw a golden glow on Teacher's body as well as on Teacher's shadow, but they disappeared in the blink of an eye. What happened?

A: That is my Law Body. I am lecturing, and I have an energy column on the top of my head; it is the state for the level I am at. It disappeared after one blink because you didn't know how to use your tianmu. You used your flesh eyes.

Q: How do we apply supernormal abilities?

A: I think it would be a problem were one to apply supernormal abilities to military science, other high technology, or espionage. Our universe has characteristics. If the usage conforms to the characteristics, the abilities work; if it doesn't, the ability will not work. Even for the purpose for doing good deeds, one might not be able to acquire things from high levels. He might only be able to sense or feel them. It doesn't do much harm to society's normal course of development if the person only uses minor supernormal abilities. If he wants to change certain things, he has to make significant efforts. In terms of whether or not he's needed for that, what he says doesn't count since the development of the society does not go according to his will. He might want to achieve certain things, but the final decision is not up to him.

Q: How does one's consciousness go in and out of the body?

A: The consciousness we talk about usually goes out through the crown of the head. Of course, it's not limited to going that way. It can go out through any spot, unlike what's emphasized in other cultivation schools, where it has to go out through the crown of the head. It can leave the body at any location. It's the same when it enters the body.

Q: There is red light in the area of tianmu with a black hole in the middle. It blooms rapidly. Is tianmu being opened? Sometimes it's also accompanied by starlight and lightning.

A: When you see starlight, the tianmu is close to being opened. When you see lightning, it is almost entirely opened.

Q: I saw red and green colored halos on Teacher's head and body. But when I closed my eyes, I couldn't see anything. Did I see with peripheral vision?

A: You didn't use peripheral vision. You just didn't know how to see with your eyes closed, so you could only do it with your eyes open. People often don't know how to use their already-opened tianmu. Sometimes they accidentally see things with their eyes open. But when you want to take a really good look at things, you actually start to use your eyes; so things disappear again. When you aren't paying attention, you will see them again.

Q: My daughter sees some circles in the sky, but she can't explain it clearly. We asked her to take a look at the Falun emblem, and she says that's what it is. Is her tianmu really open?

A: Children under the age of six can have their tianmu opened with just one glance at our Falun emblem. Nonetheless, you shouldn't do that. Children can see it.

Q: I don't know how to use the already-opened tianmu. Would Master please explain?

A: When tianmu is completely opened, people will know how to use it, even if they didn't before. When it is very bright and easy to use, people will know how to use it, even if they previously didn't. Vision through the tianmu takes place unintentionally. When you want to take a more careful look, you've inadvertently switched to your eyes and used the optic nerve. Therefore, you can't see it anymore.

Q: When tianmu is open, do we get to see the entire universe?

A: There are levels when it comes to opening tianmu. In other words, how much truth you see depends on your level. The opening of your tianmu doesn't mean that you will be able to see everything in the universe. But you will gradually improve your level through further cultivation up until you reach enlightenment. Then you will be able to see more levels. Yet even then it's not guaranteed that what you see is the truth of the entire universe. Because when Sakyamuni was preaching during his lifetime he was also continuously improving himself, every time he reached a new level he would discover that what he had lectured on previously was not definite. His lectures would change again at an even higher level. That was why he finally said, "There is no Dharma that is definitive." Each level has its own principle. It was impossible for even him to perceive the truth of the entire universe. From the standpoint of our average people, it becomes inconceivable that someone in this world can cultivate to the level of Tathagata. Because they only know of the Tathagata level and they don't know that there are levels still higher, they can no longer know or accept things of a higher nature. Tathagata is a very minor level of the Buddha Fa. This is what's referred to by the saying, "The great Fa is boundless".

Q: Do the things that we see on your body really exist?

A: Of course they really exist—all dimensions are composed of matter. It's only that their structure is different from ours.

Q: My premonitions about the future frequently come true.

A: This is the supernormal ability of "prediction" that we've talked about. In fact, it is the lower level of precognition and retrocognition *(suming tong)*. The gong we cultivate is in a different dimension where there's no concept of time or space; it is the same no matter how far the distance or how long the time.

Q: Why do colorful people, the sky, and images appear during practice?

174

A: Your tianmu has been opened, and what you saw belongs to another dimension. That dimension is layered, so you might have seen one of its levels. It is this beautiful.

Q: I heard a loud sound during practice and felt as if my body had been cracked open. I suddenly understood many things. Why?

A: It's easier for some to experience this, which is a process whereby part of the body is exploded and opened. You reached enlightenment in some regards. This is classified as gradual enlightenment. When you are finished with one of your cultivation levels, a portion of it will be exploded and opened. This is all very normal.

Q: At times, I feel that I can't move. Why is that?

A: During the initial stage of cultivation, you may feel that you suddenly can't move your hand or a particular part of your body. Why is that? It's because you have acquired a type of supernormal ability called "freeze gong." This is one of your innate abilities, and it is very powerful. When someone has committed wrongdoing and is running away, you can say "freeze" and he will instantly be frozen still.

Q: When can we start giving treatments to others? I used to treat others' sicknesses with some effectiveness. After I've learned Falun Gong, if people come to me for treatments, can I treat them?

A: I think that for people in this class—regardless of what kind of exercises you've practiced, how long you've practiced them, or whether or not you've reached the level of being able to cure disease—at this lower level, I don't want you to treat people since you don't even know yourself what state you are in. Perhaps you've healed diseases for other people. It might have been because you had a righteous mind that helped. Also, it could have been a passing-by master who gave you a hand since you were doing a good deed. Despite the fact that the energy you've developed through cultivation helps you to do something, it cannot protect you. When you give a treatment you are in the same field as the patient. Over the course of time, the patient's black qi will make you sicker than he. If you asked the patient, "Are you recovered?" he would say, "A little better." What kind of treatment is that? Some qigong masters say: "Come back tomorrow and again the day after tomorrow. I'll treat you for a few sessions." He also does it in "cycles." Isn't that deceitful? Won't it be wonderful if you can hold off on treating disease until you reach a higher level? Whoever you treat will recover. How good that will feel! If you've already developed gong at a not-so-low level, and if it's absolutely necessary that you give a treatment, I will open your hands and bring out your supernormal ability of curing diseases. But if you're to cultivate toward higher levels, I think it's best that you stay away from these things. In order to promote the Great Law *(Dafa)* and participate in social events, some of my disciples are giving treatments. Because they are by my side and being trained by me, they are protected and it's not going to cause problems.

Q: Can we tell others if we've developed supernormal abilities?

A: It's not a problem if you tell others who also practice Falun Gong, provided that you're modest. The reason for having all of you practice together is so that you can exchange and discuss. Of course, if you run into outside people who possess supernormal abilities, you can also tell them. It doesn't really matter as long as you don't brag. If you want to brag about how capable you are, that will create problems. If you've bragged for a long while, the ability will disappear. If you only want to talk about qigong phenomena and discuss without any inappropriate personal thoughts, I'd say that won't be a problem.

Q: The Buddha School talks about "emptiness" while the Tao School "nothingness." What do we talk about?

A: The Buddha School's "emptiness" and the Tao School's "nothingness" are unique to their own cultivation methods. Of course, we are also required to reach that level. We talk about cultivating intentionally and acquiring gong unintentionally. Cultivating your xinxing and abandoning attachments also results in emptiness and nothingness, but we don't emphasize those as heavily. Because you live in the material world, you need to make a living and have a career—you have to do things. Doing things inevitably brings about the issue of whether what you do is a good thing or a bad one. What should we do? What we cultivate is xinxing, the most prominent feature of our method. As long as your mind is righteous and the things you do meet our requirements, there will be no problem with your xinxing.

Q: How do we sense the development of our supernormal abilities?

A: During the initial stage of cultivation, if you've developed supernormal abilities you will be able to feel it. If you haven't yet developed supernormal abilities but your body is sensitive, you might be able to feel it. If neither is happening, there is no way for you to tell. The only thing you can do is to continue to cultivate without awareness of them. There are sixty to seventy percent of our students who have their tianmu open. I know they can see. Though you don't say anything, you observe with your eyes wide open. Why do I ask you to practice together? I want you to exchange and discuss internally within your groups. But to be responsible to this cultivation method, you should not talk without restraint outside of the group. Internal exchange and improving each other is acceptable.

Q: What does the Law Body look like? Do I have Law Bodies?

A: A person's Law Body looks the same as that person. You don't have Law Bodies now. When your cultivation reaches a certain level, you will be finished with In-Triple-World-Law cultivation and enter an extremely high level. Only then will you develop Law Bodies.

Q: After the class is finished, for how long will Teacher's Law Bodies follow us?

A: When a student suddenly starts to cultivate things of higher levels, this represents a big turning point for him. It doesn't refer to changes in his thinking, but to his entire person. So when an everyday person gets what he's not supposed to get as an everyday person, it becomes dangerous, his life will be threatened. My Law Bodies must provide him with protection. If I couldn't do this yet still spread the Fa, it would be the same as harming people. Many qigong masters are afraid of teaching cultivation and doing this, because they cannot handle the responsibility. My Law Bodies will protect you all the time until you reach enlightenment. If you stop halfway, the Law Bodies will, of their own accord, simply leave you.

178

Q: Teacher says, "People with average inborn quality cultivate not through exercises, but through xinxing." Is it correct to say that as long as one's xinxing is very high, one can attain the Right Fruit without practicing the exercise?

A: Theoretically it's correct. As long as you cultivate your xinxing, de can be transformed into gong. But you must regard yourself as a cultivator. If you don't, the only thing you can achieve is continued accumulation of de. You might be able to amass a great deal of de, persisting in being a righteous person to accumulate de. In that case, even if you regarded yourself as a cultivator you wouldn't be able to go further, as you wouldn't have learned the Fa of higher levels. As all of you know, I've disclosed many things. Without Teacher's protection, it's very hard to cultivate to higher levels. It would be impossible for you to cultivate at higher levels—even for one day. Therefore, reaching enlightenment isn't that easy. But after your xinxing has been improved, you can assimilate to the characteristics of the universe.

Q: What is the principle behind remote treatment?

A: It's very simple. The universe can expand or shrink; so can supernormal abilities. I remain in the original location and don't move, but the supernormal abilities that have been emitted can reach patients as far away as in the United States. [To treat a person], I can either release supernormal abilities to his place or directly summon his essential spirit *(yuanshen)* to come here. This is the principle of remote treatment.

Q: Can we know how many kinds of supernormal abilities will be developed?

A: There are more than ten thousand types of supernormal abilities. It's not important to know in detail exactly how many. Knowing this principle and this Fa is sufficient. The remainder is left for you to cultivate. Knowing that much is neither necessary nor good for you. Masters look for disciples and accept disciples. Those disciples don't know anything at all, and neither will their masters tell them. It's all up to them to realize for themselves.

Q: When I close my eyes in class I can see you lecturing on the stage. Your upper body is black. The desk is black, too. The cloth behind you is pink. Sometimes you are surrounded by green light. What's going on?

A: This is an issue of the level you're at, for when the tianmu is just opened you will perceive white as black and black as white. After your level has improved a bit, everything you see will be white. After yet further improvement, you can differentiate all colors.

5. Tribulations

Q: Are tribulations tests arranged by Master for the students?

A: You could say that. These are planned to improve your xinxing. Suppose your xinxing hasn't reached the required level, will you be allowed to reach enlightenment and complete your cultivation? Does it work if we send an elementary school student to college? I don't think so! If we let you cultivate to a higher level when your xinxing hasn't been truly improved and you still can't lighten your view on anything or forgo anything, you might argue with the enlightened ones over trivial things. That's unacceptable! This is why we put so much emphasis on xinxing.

Q: What's the difference between cultivators' tribulations and those of everyday people?

A: We cultivators aren't much different from everyday people. Your tribulations are arranged according to your path as a cultivator. Since everyday people are paying for the karma of everyday people, all of them have tribulations. It doesn't mean that since you're a cultivator you will have tribulations, and that since he's an everyday person he won't. It's the same in both scenarios. It's just that your tribulations are orchestrated for the purpose of improving your xinxing, whereas his tribulations have been orchestrated to pay his karmic debt. The truth of the matter is that tribulations are your own karma that I utilize to improve a disciples' xinxing.

Q: Are tribulations similar to those eighty-one hardships that occurred on the journey to the West to get the scriptures?[72]

A: There is a little similarity. The lives of cultivators have been prearranged. You won't have too many or too few hardships, and there won't necessarily be eighty-one of them. It depends on how high you can cultivate to with your inborn quality; this has been planned according to the level you might achieve. Cultivators will experience the process of abandoning everything that everyday people have but that cultivators should not. It is indeed tough. We will think of ways to make you give up all the things you find hard to relinquish, therefore improving your xinxing

---

[72] A story in the classic work of Chinese fiction, <u>Journey to the West.</u>

through tribulations.

Q: What if when we practice there are people who try to sabotage it?

A: Falun Gong doesn't fear sabotage by other people. At the initial stage you have my Law Bodies protecting you, but it's not certain that you won't encounter anything. It's impossible to develop gong by sitting on a couch drinking tea all day. Sometimes when you encounter tribulations you call out my name and see me right in front of you. I might not assist you, because that is what you need to overcome. But when you are truly in danger, I will help you. Nevertheless, real danger normally doesn't exist since your path has been changed and nothing accidental is allowed to intervene.

Q: How should we deal with tribulations?

A: I have emphasized it repeatedly: guard your xinxing! If you can ensure that you don't do the wrong things, then that is good. It is especially important when others infringe upon your interests for certain reasons: if you fight back like an everyday person, you, too, will become an everyday person. Because you're a cultivator you shouldn't handle things that way. The things that interfere with xinxing which you run into are to improve your xinxing. It all depends on how you deal with them and whether you maintain and improve your xinxing from this matter.

6. Dimensions and Humankind

Q: How many levels of dimensions are there in the universe?

A: According to what I know, the number of layers of dimensions in the universe is innumerable. When it comes to the existence of various other dimensions, what exists in those dimensions, and who lives there, it's very hard to know using current scientific means. Modern science has yet to produce material proof. Yet some of our qigong masters and people who possess supernormal abilities can see other dimensions. This is because other dimensions can only be seen by tianmu, and not by the human flesh eye.

Q: Does every dimension embrace the characteristics of Zhen, Shan, and Ren?

A: Yes, every dimension embraces the characteristics of Zhen, Shan, and Ren. People conforming to these characteristics are good people, while those going against them are bad. Those who assimilate to it are enlightened.

Q: Where did the original mankind come from?

A: The original universe didn't have as many vertical or horizontal levels. It was quite pure. Over the course of its development and movement, life was generated. That was what we called the most original life. It was in conformity with the universe, and nothing bad existed. Being in conformity with the universe means that it was the same as the universe, having whatever capabilities the universe had. As the universe was developing and evolving, some heavenly paradises appeared. Later, more and more lives appeared.

183

Speaking with the terms at our low level, social groups were formed in which mutual interactions developed. During this evolutionary process, some people changed, deviating further away from the characteristics of the universe. They became not as good, so their divine powers weakened. Cultivators thus stress "returning to truthfulness," which means returning to the original state. The higher the level, the more assimilated it is to the universe and the more powerful the abilities are. At that time, some lives became bad during the universe's evolution, and yet they couldn't be destroyed. Therefore, plans were made so that they could improve themselves and assimilate again to the universe. They were sent to a lower level to bear some sufferings and improve themselves. Later, people continuously came to this level. Then a division happened at this level. People whose xinxing had deteriorated could no longer remain at this level. So another, even lower level was created. It went on like this with lower and lower levels gradually getting differentiated, until the level that today's mankind occupies was generated. This is the origin of today's mankind.

List of Falun Dafa Books in English

Zhuan Falun

China Falun Gong

Falun Dafa—Essentials for Further Advancement

Falun Dafa Lectures in the United States

For more information on Falun Dafa books and materials, please visit The Universe Publishing Company's website at

http://www.universepublishing.com

─ ─ ─ ─ ─ ─ ─ ─ ─ ─ ─ ─ ─ ─ ─ ─ ─ ─ ─

Free Instruction and Workshops Worldwide

Falun Dafa practitioners provide free instruction and workshops worldwide. Books in different languages are available on Internet for free download. For further information, please visit the following websites:

http://www.falundafa.org (USA)

http://www.falundafa.ca (Canada)

http://www.falundafa.au (Australia)

or call toll free: **1-877-FALUN99 (North America)**

Falun Dafa Books and Tapes Order Form

TO: **The Universe Publishing Company**
P. O. Box 2026
New York, NY 10013
Tel: (212) 343-3056 Fax: (212) 343-9512
E-mail:order@universepublishing.com
WebSite: www.universepublishing.com

Name: **E-mail (if any):**
Telephone: **Fax (if any):**
Address:

Shipping Address (if different from above):

ISBN and Description	Unit Price	Qty.	Total
1-58613-100-1 China Falun Gong (English)	$12.95	____	____
1-58613-101-X Zhuan Falun (English)	$12.95	____	____
1-58613-403-5 Falun Dafa Exercise Instruction Video Tape (English, 60min.)	$12.00	____	____

SubTotal: _____

NY Sales Tax 8.25% (For New York Residents Only): _____

(Individuals add $2 per item for shipping) Shipping: _____

Grand Total: _____

Please make your check or money order payable to:
The Universe Publishing Company
P. O. Box 2026
New York, NY 10013

186

way. As a result, they want to attach themselves to human bodies and acquire the human essence. There is also another rule in this universe, namely: no loss, no gain. They thus want to satisfy your desire for fame and personal gain. They make you rich and famous, but they don't help you for nothing. They also want to gain something—your essence. When they leave you, you will have nothing left and turn very weak or become a vegetable. This is caused by a crooked xinxing. One right mind will subdue a hundred evils. When you are righteous, you will not attract evil. In other words, be a noble practitioner, turn away from all nonsense, and only cultivate the righteous way.

(6) An Evil Way can be Produced in Righteous Practice

Although the gong learned by some people comes from righteous cultivation ways, people can actually inadvertently practice evil ways since they are unable to impose strict self-requirements, fail to cultivate xinxing, and entertain negative thoughts during practice. For example, when a person is practicing there, either in the standing stance or the sitting exercise, his thoughts are actually on money and personal gain, "He's wronged me, and I'll fix him after I acquire supernormal abilities." Or he is thinking of this or that supernormal ability, adding something very bad to his gong and actually practicing an evil way. This is very dangerous, as it may attract some very negative things, such as low-level beings. Perhaps the person doesn't even know he has invited them. Because his attachment is strong—purposefully practicing cultivation to fulfill desires is unacceptable—he isn't righteous, and even his master will be unable to protect him. Therefore, practitioners must maintain their xinxing strictly, keeping a righteous mind and craving nothing. Otherwise, problems might arise.

32

this energy is dispersed, it has very little power. It is effective in treating minor sickness, but fails with serious illness. Buddhism speaks of how people above lack suffering and conflict, and how they therefore cannot cultivate; furthermore, they cannot temper themselves and are unable to improve their levels. They thus look for ways to help people gain better health, thereby improving themselves. This is what the cosmic language is all about. The cosmic language is not a supernormal ability, and neither is it qigong.

(5) Spirit Possession

The most injurious type of spirit possession is possession by a low-level being; this is caused by cultivating an evil way. It is very harmful to people, and the consequences of people being possessed are frightening. Not long after practicing, some people become obsessed with becoming rich; they think of these things all the time. Originally, these people might have been pretty decent or might have already had a master looking after them. Nevertheless, things turn sour when they start to contemplate giving treatments and getting rich. They then attract this type of being. It is not in our material dimension, and yet it truly exists.

Such a practitioner suddenly feels that his tianmu is open and that he now has gong, but it is actually the possessing spirit that has control of his brain. It reflects the images that it sees onto the person's brain, making him feel that his tianmu has been opened. Actually, his tianmu has not been opened whatsoever. Why does the possessing spirit want to give him gong? Why does it want to help him? It is because animals are forbidden to cultivate in our universe. Since animals know nothing about xinxing and cannot improve themselves, they are not allowed to obtain the righteous